ABOLITION DEMOCRACY

BEYOND EMPIRE, PRISONS, AND TORTURE

Interviews with Angela Y. Davis

SEVEN STORIES PRESS

NEW YORK

Seven Stories Press
140 Watts Street
New York, NY 10013
www.sevenstories.com

Library of Congress Cataloging-in-Publication Data

Davis, Angela Y. (Angela Yvonne), 1944-
  Abolition democracy : beyond empire, prisons, and torture / interviews with Angela Y. Davis.-- 1st ed.
    p. cm.
  ISBN: 978-1-58322-695-7 (pbk. : alk. paper)
  1. African Americans--Civil rights--History. 2. African Americans--Violence against. 3. Political prisoners--Abuse of.--United States. 4. Torture--United States. 5. United States--Race relations. I. Title.
E185.61.D38 2005
323.0973'090511--dc22   2005030346

College professors may order examination copies of Seven Stories Press titles for a free six-month trial period. To order, visit www.sevenstories.com/textbook or fax on school letterhead to (212) 226-1411.

Book design by Jon Gilbert

Cover design and photo by Greg Ruggiero

Printed in the USA.

19 18 17 16

Contents

Introduction

BY EDUARDO MENDIETA

Angela Y. Davis is known by many as the iconic face of 1970s Black Pride. Others know her as the former vice-presidential candidate of the Communist Party of the United States, while others know her as a major feminist scholar who has written some of the most transformative and enduring texts of feminist thinking in the last quarter century. And a new generation of students, activists and cultural workers got to know her in 1997 when Professor Davis helped found Critical Resistance, a national organization dedicated to dismantling the prison-industrial-complex, a topic that is central to her current scholarship and activism. In fact, throughout each of her life's projects Angela Y. Davis has been an unwavering prison activist whose focus has returned repeatedly to the opposition of prisons, imprisonment and racialized punishment.

Vladimir I. Lenin claimed that prisons are the universities of revolutionaries, and while Angela Davis was already a revolutionary by the time she was placed on the FBI's Ten Most Wanted List on false charges, driven underground, arrested, and incarcerated, her work has been indelibly marked by her experience of imprisonment.[1] Some of her earliest published works were written during her sixteen-month incarceration, brilliant pieces in which she established the links between surplus repression, punishment, and the racial violence at the heart of white supremacy in the United States.

Reading Davis, one is immediately struck by her sources, starting with her own experience as a black women, political prisoner, and American citizen who was at one time labeled an "enemy of the state" only to then become the focus of an intense international solidarity movement—the "Free Angela Davis" campaign—that lead to her acquittal in 1972. Another source is her continuous engagement with the canonical figures in what one can call a tradition of black critical political philosophy that has found two towering figures in Frederick Douglass and W. E. B. DuBois. This engagement harkens back to her early seventies *Lectures on Liberation*, in which we find a neo-Marxist, or Frankfurt School approach to the thought of Douglass.[2] In one of the essays that Davis wrote while she was in the Marin County Jail, Davis turns to DuBois—for it is in him that she found the most severe and explicit critique of the prison system in the United States. It is in DuBois, furthermore, that Davis discerns the historical links between slavery, the failed reconstruction, the turn of the century lynchings, the emergence of the KKK, Jim Crow, the riots of the post-civil war period, and the rise of the racial ghettos in all major U.S. cities.

It is important to underscore Davis's engagement with Douglass's and DuBois's work, for both stand in for two philosophical approaches in Davis's thinking, approaches that must be juxtaposed against one another. On the one hand, Douglass represents an existential concern with freedom that easily translates into a deference to political liberty in terms of voting rights. Indeed, in a 1995 essay entitled "From the Prison of Slavery to the Slavery of Prison: Frederick Douglass and the Convict Lease System,"[3] Davis presents a devastating critique of Douglass's myopia and inability to both speak out and mobilize around what was obviously a betrayal of the political freedom won by blacks. Shortly after the Civil War the south underwent a process of democratization that was awe-inspiring and utopian, although tragically short-lived. Union troops were stationed in the South to make sure that blacks would be protected while going to the voting polls. Blacks were elected as senators. Schools were opened. A vibrant black public sphere began to emerge. This short-lived period came to be known as the "Reconstruction." Within a decade, however, the reconstruction had been halted and a process of retreat back towards slavery began. White legislators mandated a series of laws that forced black freed men to become indentured servants by criminalizing them. The prerogatives of former white slave owners were legislated and legalized in the infamous "Blacks Laws." Once in prison, convicts were leased or rented for absurd fees to the private entrepreneurs of the new South. This process became known as the convict leasing system, and historians have gone so far as to say that it was "worse than slavery."[4]

The black laws of the south turned black free men into criminals so that their labor could be exploited even more pugnaciously and rapaciously than when they had been slaves. The convict leasing system became one of the most lucrative mechanisms for simultaneous control, along with gerrymandering of black free labor and extreme exploitation. DuBois put it this way:

> This penitentiary system [the prison leasing system] began to characterize the whole South. In Georgia, at the outbreak of the Civil War, there were about 200 white felons confined at Milledgeville. There were no Negro convicts, since under the discipline of slavery, Negroes were punished in the plantation. The white convicts were released to fight in the Confederate armies. The whole criminal system came to be used as a method of keeping Negroes at work and intimidating them. Consequently there began to be a demand for jails and penitentiaries beyond the natural demand due to the rise of crime.[5]

According to historians, precious little is known of Douglass's views on the "convict leasing system." Davis critiques Douglass's loud silence on this matter because it was surely a nightmare that most blacks in post-Civil War America lived and experienced first hand. Douglass, in Davis's view, may have been blinded to this reality because he was so thoroughly focused on getting the ballot for blacks that in the process he entirely neglected the economic well being of blacks. For Davis, "[c]onvict leasing was a totalitarian effort to control black labor in the post-Emancipation era and it served fully as a *symbolic reminder* to black people that slavery had not been fully disestablished."[6] Davis also faults Douglass for his overconfidence in the law as an allegedly dispassionate and impartial tool that could not be used to roll back the gains of the post-emancipation period. As an enlightenment thinker, Douglass saw law as a mechanism to bring about justice and democracy for black Americans but failed to see how it could be used—and *was* used—to brand black human beings as criminals.

In contrast, Davis turns to DuBois as the exemplar political thinker, even as Davis also acknowledges the pioneering work of D. E. Tobias and Mary Church Terrell, two other black scholars who studied and documented the devastating effects of the prison leasing system. In DuBois, Davis finds a critique of Douglass's naïve trust in both the economic and political independence of post-slavery blacks as well as a critique of the ways in which the state was a direct party to preservation and mutation of slavery. DuBois saw clearly how the state participates in the criminalization of blacks so that their labor could be extracted through the mechanism of the prison leasing system. As DuBois put it in his monumental *Black Reconstruction,*

> In no part of the modern world has there been so open and conscious a traffic in crime for deliberate social degradation and private profit as in the South since

slavery. The Negro is not anti-social. He is no natural criminal. Crime of the vicious type, outside endeavor to achieve freedom or in revenge for cruelty, was rare in the slave south. Since 1876 Negroes have been arrested on the slightest provocation and given long sentences or fines that they were compelled to work for as if they were slaves or indentured servants again. The resulting peonage of criminals extended into every Southern state and led to the most revolting situations.[7]

For DuBois, black labor was neither economically free nor politically self-determining. Thus, blacks entered a racialized public sphere of American democracy as disadvantaged and unequal. Democracy for blacks had been withheld at the very moment it had been promised: upon the abolition of slavery. With the abolition of slavery blacks ceased to be slaves, but immediately became criminals—and as criminals, they became slaves of the state. Thus, DuBois represents for Davis an anti-capitalist, antistatist, antilaw perspective that is profoundly attentive to what we can call the social imaginary, or civic imagination.

Davis, however, is neither an exegete nor historian. She is an original radical thinker, whose contributions to an emerging theory of penality are used in the classroom as much as they are by activists and community organizers. In the context of this short introduction we only have space to give the general shape and main lines of argument in Davis's thinking, which I think can be discussed in terms the following themes:

DISENFRANCHISEMENT

For Davis, one of the functions of the prison-industrial-complex is to withhold the vote from people of color. All fifty U.S. states bar former inmates from acquiring state licenses. This means that they are *de facto* excluded from many, if not most, jobs. A total of seven states permanently disenfranchise formerly incarcerated persons. Seven additional states also disenfranchise certain types of former incarcerated persons (which is determined according to the type of crime they allegedly committed), thirty-three states disenfranchise persons on parole, and forty-eight states disenfranchise persons in prisons, the sole exceptions being Maine and Vermont.

CAPITAL EXTRACTION

Davis often delves into how the prison is a mechanism of wealth extraction from African Americans not just through exploitation of prison labor, but also by appropriating black social wealth. By social wealth, Davis means the wherewithal of black Americans to sustain their communities: schools, churches, home ownership, etc. At any given moment, given the exorbitant amount of blacks in prisons, social wealth does not return to black communities, or it is withdrawn through political and economic disenfranchisement and exclusion.

SOCIAL BRANDING

Once a black American has been in prison, he or she is permanently branded. As recent studies have shown, it is more difficult for former black prisoners to regain entry into society than it is for their white counterparts.

RACIAL CONTRACT

In Davis's thinking, the racial contract refers to the social, political, cultural and economic reality in which it is more advantageous to be white than a person of color because all norms are *de facto* whiteness norms. Within the racial contract social punishment is accepted because it is done primarily to blacks. So, we tolerate a highly punitive society because its punishment is performed on *them*, and not on *us*. For Davis, the prison-industrial-complex also contributes to the domination of racial minorities by domesticating the civic imagination of white Americans.

RITUAL VIOLENCE

In Davis's work she discusses how ritual violence cleanses and expiates the social order. The prison system naturalizes the violence that is enacted against racial minorities by institutionalizing a viciously circular logic: blacks are in prisons because they are criminals; they are criminals because they are black, and if they are in prison, they deserved what they got. Prison in more than one way institutionalized the lynchings of the turn of the 20th century, when Jim Crow was at its cruelest and most violent.

SEXUAL COERCION

Davis repeatedly returns to the fact that the prison uses sexualized abuse for social control. The aggressive masculinity of the inmates is matched by the sexual coercion enacted by the guards and wardens in prisons. In this way the prison system is a regime that is predicated on sexual violence that is at the same time highly racialized.

SURPLUS REPRESSION

Davis critiques how the institutionalization of the prison regime into an industry instills in the minds of citizens that prisons are both inevitable and desirable. They are a logical and evident way to deal with crime. We have so many prisons, because we build them, and so many sectors of society are invested in their perpetuation. Citizens, however, are not allowed to ask: Is imprisonment the only way to deal with crime and social dysfunction? Is crime really dealt with by prisons? Are the long terms costs of imprisonment worth the momentary benefits of putatively deterring crime?

INTERCONNECTED SYSTEMS

In her work on prisons, Davis often focuses on the insidious relationship between the prison-industrial-complex and the military industrial complex. Acknowledging these relationships is a necessary first step in developing strategies to oppose and abolish the institutions and their underlying causes.

For authentic democracy to emerge, Davis argues, *abolition democracy* must be enacted—the abolition of institutions that advance the dominance of any one group over any other. Abolition democracy, then, is the democracy that is to come,[8] the democracy that is possible if we continue with the great abolition movements in American history, those that opposed slavery, lynching, and segregation.[9] So long as the prison-industrial-complex remains, American democracy will continue to be a false one. Such a false democracy reduces people and their communities to the barest biological subsistence because it pushes them outside the law and the polity. Is this not what we plainly saw in New Orleans in the wake of Hurricane Katrina?

Such a bare existence is one that can be ignored and neglected, or extinguished with impunity precisely because it is the law that renders it expendable. Punishment has been deployed against the human body as though it were a black body. The death penalty survives not as the ultimate punishment, but because it was primarily a form of punishment against the black flesh and black freedom. And this is what is so indelibly announced in the Thirteenth Amendment to the Constitution. As neo-Abolitionist Joy James put it, "The Thirteenth Amendment ensnares as it emancipates. In fact, it functions as an enslaving antienslavement narrative."

The interviews in this book were all conducted by me alone, except the final one, to which Chad Kautzer, a graduate student at Stony Brook University and a peace activist, contributed. In these discussions, which took place over the span of eight months during which we were witnesses to the disclosures of torture at Guantánamo and Abu Ghraib, Angela Davis takes her analysis of the prison-industrial-complex to new levels. She focuses on the effects of the prison regime on our foreign relations, and discusses how our society seems unable to acknowledge the humanity and suffering of others, as manifested today in the people shown in the Abu Ghraib photos. The images seem to affirm for us the fiction of American democracy at the very moment that this democracy is at its weakest and most betrayed.

In analyses that are both original and poignant, Davis lays bare the links between empire, prison, and torture—analyses that will outlast our current historical moment. These interviews are immediate responses—from a former enemy of the state who has become of the most important public intellectuals—to perhaps the most intense crisis of American political and ethical identity of our time.

Politics and Prisons

Angela Davis, you are probably one of the top five most important black women in American history. In 1974, your book Angela Davis: An Autobiography *was published by Random House. Since then it has become a classic of African-American letters that is central to the traditions of black women writers and black political thinkers. In many ways your autobiography also harkens back to the tradition of black slave narratives. How do you see this work now with thirty years hindsight?*

Well, thanks for reminding me that this is the thirtieth anniversary of the publication of my autobiography. At the time I wrote the book I did not see myself as a conventional autobiographical subject and thus did not locate my writing within any of the traditions you evoke. As a matter of fact, I was initially reluctant to write an autobiography. First of all, I was too young. Second, I did not think that my own individual accomplishments merited autobiographical treatment. Third, I was certainly aware that the celebrity—or notoriety—I had achieved had very little to do with me as an individual. It was based on the mobilization of the State and its efforts to capture me, including the fact that I was placed on the FBI's Ten Most Wanted list. But also, and perhaps most importantly, I knew that my potential as an autobiographical subject was created by the massive global movement that successfully achieved my freedom. So the question was how to write an autobiography that would be attentive to this community of collective struggle. I decided then that I did not want to write a conventional autobiography in which the heroic subject offers lessons to readers. I decided that I would write a political autobiography exploring the way in which I had been shaped by movements and campaigns in communities of struggle. In this sense, you can certainly say that I wrote myself into the tradition of black slave narratives.

In what way do you think that the black political biography plays a role within this tradition of American letters?

Well of course the canon of American letters has been contested previously, and if one considers the autobiography of Malcolm X as an example, which, along with literature by such writers as Zora Neale Hurston, Alice Walker, and Toni Morrison, that has clearly made its way into the canon, one can ask whether the inclusion of oppositional writing has really made a difference. Has the canon itself has been substantively transformed? It seems to me that struggles to contest bodies of literature are similar to the struggles for social change and social transformation. What we manage to do each time we win a victory is not so much to secure change once and for all, but rather to create new terrains for struggle.

Since we are talking about canons, it seems to me that your work fits within another tradition—the philosophical canon. If we think of the work of Boethius, of Jean-Paul Sartre, Martin Luther King, Dietrich Bonhoeffer, Antonio Gramsci, Primo Levi . . . these are philosophical figures who have reflected upon their prison experiences. Do you see your work contributing to this philosophical tradition of prison writing, and if so, how?

Well, often times prison writing is described as that which is produced in prison or by prisoners, and certainly Gramsci's prison notebooks provide the most interesting example. It is significant that Gramsci's prison letters have not received the consideration they deserve. It would be interesting to read Gramsci's letters alongside those of George Jackson. These are two examples of prison intellectuals who devoted some of their energies to the process of engaging critically with the implications of imprisonment—at a more concrete philosophical level. Personally, I found it rather difficult to think critically about the prison while I was a prisoner. So I suppose I follow in the tradition of some of the thinkers you mention. However, I did publish a piece while I was in jail that could be considered a more indirect examination of issues related to imprisonment. I wrote an article entitled "Reflections on the Black Woman's Role in the Community of Slaves,"[10] which helped me formulate some of the questions that I would later take up in my efforts to theorize the relationship between the institution of the prison and that of slavery. I produced another piece—a paper I wrote for the conference for the Society for the Study of Dialectical Materialism, associated with the American Philosophical Association—entitled "Women and Capitalism: Dialectics of Oppression and Liberation." Both pieces were published in *The Angela Y. Davis Reader* in 1998. *If They Come in the Morning,* the book on political prisoners I wrote and edited with Bettina Aptheker, is another example of my prison writing. Finally, I also wrote an extended study of fascism which was never published. But it was only after I was released that I felt I had sufficient critical distance to think more deeply about the institution of the prison, drawing from and extending the work of the prison intellectual George Jackson.

You were trained as a philosopher, yet you teach in a program called the History of Consciousness at the University of California. Do you think that philosophy can play a role in political culture in the United States? And, has philosophy influenced your work on aesthetics, jazz, and in particular, the way in which you analyze the situation of black women?

Absolutely, and I think that I draw from my background in philosophy in that I try to ask questions about contemporary and historical realities that tend to be otherwise fore-closed. Philosophy provides a vantage point from which to ask questions that cannot be posed within social scientific discourse that presumes to furnish overarching frameworks for understanding of our social world. I have learned a great deal from Herbert Marcuse about the relationship between philosophy and ideology critique. I draw particular inspiration from his work *Counterrevolution and Revolt* that attempts to directly theorize political developments of the late 1960s. But at the same time the framework is philosophical. How do we imagine a better world and raise the questions that permit us to see beyond the given?

There are beautiful pages in your autobiography about your relationship with Herbert Marcuse, who was your teacher and mentor, and part of the Frankfurt School. You spent some years in Frankfurt in the late 1960s. You also studied with Theodor Adorno, Jürgen Habermas, and Max Horkheimer. Do you see yourself as a critical theorist in this Frankfurt School sense?

Well, I've certainly been inspired by critical theory, which privileges the role of philosophical reflection while simultaneously recognizing that philosophy cannot always by itself generate the answers to the questions it poses. When philosophical inquiry enters into conversation with other disciplines and methods, we are able to produce much more fruitful results. Marcuse crossed the disciplinary borders that separate philosophy, sociology, and literature. Adorno brought music and philosophy into the conversation. These were some of the first serious efforts to legitimate interdisciplinary inquiry.

You ran twice as the vice-presidential candidate of the Communist Party in the United States before leaving the party in the 1990s. After the fall of the Berlin wall and the demise of the Soviet Union, what role, if any, can communism play today?

Although I am no longer a member of the Communist Party, I still consider myself a communist. If I did not believe in the possibility of eventually defeating capitalism and in a socialist future, I would have no inspiration to continue with my political work. As triumphant as capitalism is assumed to be in the aftermath of the collapse of the socialist community of nations, it also continually reveals its inability to grow and develop without expanding and deepening human exploitation. There must be an alternative to capitalism. Today, the tendency to assume that the only version of democracy available to us is capitalist democracy poses a challenge. We must be able to disentangle our notions of capitalism and democracy so to pursue truly egalitarian models of democracy. Communism—or socialism—can still help us to generate new versions of democracy.

Do you think that the anti-globalization movement—the anti-WTO movement—can take up the role that Karl Marx assigned to the proletariat? In other words, can we say, "anti-globalists of the world unite"?

Well, this transition is a little too easy. But this is not to dismiss the importance of creating global solidarities, cross-racial solidarities attentive to struggles against economic exploitation, racism, patriarchy, and homophobia. And there is a link, it seems to me, between the internationalism of Karl Marx's era and the new globalisms we are seeking to build today. Of course, the global economy is far more complicated than Marx could ever imagine. But at the same time his analyses have important contemporary resonances. The entire trajectory of Capital is initiated by an examination of the commodity, that seemingly simple unit of the capitalist political economy. As it turns out, of course, the commodity is a mysterious thing. And perhaps even more mysterious today than during Marx's times. The commodity has penetrated every aspect of people's lives all over the world in ways that have no historical precedent. The commodity—and capitalism in general—has insinuated itself into structures of feeling, into the most intimate spaces of people's lives. At the same time human beings are more connected than ever before and in ways we rarely acknowledge. I am thinking of a song performed by Sweet Honey and the Rock about the global assembly line, which links us in ways contingent on exploitative practices of production and consumption. In the Global North, we purchase the pain and exploitation of girls in the Global South, which we wear everyday on our bodies.

The sweatshops of the world.

The global sweatshops. And the challenge is, as Marx argued long ago, to uncover the social relations that are both embodied and concealed by these commodities.

There is a great tradition of African-American political thought that has been deeply influenced by Marxism and communism. But one way that we sometimes talk about black political thought is in terms of two figures in tension. For example, there are the comparisons made by John Brown versus Frederick Douglass; Booker T. Washington versus W. E. B. Du Bois; Malcom X versus Martin Luther King. And in this we are able to discuss the tensions between black nationalism and assimilation or integration. How do you see yourself in relationship to the tension between nationalism and integration?

Well, of course it is possible to think about black history as it has been shaped by these debates in various eras. And we shouldn't forget the debate between W. E. B. Du Bois and Marcus Garvey. But I actually am interested in that which is foreclosed by the conceptualization of the major issues of black history in terms of these debates between black men. And I say men because the women always tend to be excluded. Where, for example, do Anna Julia Cooper and Ida B. Wells stand in these debates? But I am interested precisely in what gets foreclosed by this tension between nationalism and integration. And perhaps not primarily because the actors are male, but because questions regarding gender and sexuality are foreclosed.

So you see your work as contesting this way of viewing the black tradition of political thought . . .

Yes.

. . . that way of making sense of integration.

Exactly.

So you wanted to displace the focus and say there's another way in which black political thought can proceed.

Absolutely, and I think that the assumption today that black political thought must either advocate nationalism or must disavow black formations and black culture is very misleading.

Yes, but one of the things that is attributed to globalization is the end of nationalisms. Do you think that there is a role for black nationalism in the United States? Has it become entirely obsolete, an anachronism?

Well, in one sense it has become obsolete, but in another sense one can argue that the nationalisms that have helped to shape black consciousness will endure. First of all, I should say that I don't think that nationalism is a homogeneous concept. There are many versions of nationalism. I've always preferred to identify with the pan-Africanism of W. E. B. Du Bois who argued that black people in the West do have a special responsibility to Africa, Latina America, and Asia—not by virtue of a biological connection or a racial link, but by virtue of a political identification that is forged in struggle. We should be attentive to Africa not simply because this continent is populated by black people, not only because we trace our origins to Africa, but primarily because Africa has been a major target of colonialism and imperialism. What I also like about Du Bois's pan-Africanism is that it insists on Afro-Asian solidarities. This is an important feature that has been concealed in conventional narratives of pan-Africanism. Such an approach is not racially defined, but rather discovers its political identity in its struggles against racism.

In addition to the recent thirtieth anniversary of your autobiography, we are also celebrating fifty-plus years of Brown v. Board of Education. *Do you think that the forces of black integration, the forces of civil rights, have been betrayed and somehow rolled-back by the past two decades of Rehnquist serving as the Reagan-appointed chief justice?*

The promise of those struggles has been betrayed. But I don't think it is helpful to assume that an agenda that gets established at one point in history will forever claim success on the basis of its initial victories. It is misleading to assume that this success will be enduring, that it will survive all of the changes and mutations of the future. The civil rights movement managed to bring about enormous political shifts, which opened doors to people previously excluded from government, corporations, education, housing, etc. However, an exclusively civil rights approach—as even Dr. King recognized before he died—cannot by itself eliminate structural racism. What the civil rights movement did, it seems to me, was to create a new terrain for asking new questions and moving in new directions. The assumption that the placement of black people like Colin Powell and Condoleezza Rice in the heart of government would mean progress for the entire community was clearly fallacious. In this, there were no guarantees, to borrow from Stuart Hall. The civil rights movement demanded access, and access has been granted to some. The challenge of the twenty-first century is not to demand equal opportunity to participate in the machinery of oppression. Rather, it is to identify and dismantle those structures in which racism continues to be embedded. This is the only way the promise of freedom can be extended to masses of people.

But don't you worry about the conservative court? I mean if we think about the role of the Warren Court in advancing the racial justice agenda . . .

Oh, absolutely!

The justices in today's Supreme Court are very outspoken about their conservatism. What does this mean for racial justice in the future?

Of course I'm worried about that. The only point I'm attempting to make is that past struggles cannot correct current injustices and that people who tend to sit back and bemoan the betrayal of the civil rights movement are not prepared to imagine what might be necessary at *this* moment to challenge the conservatism of the Supreme Court. It's very difficult to recognize contemporary racisms, especially when they are not linked to racist laws and attitudes and when they differently affect individuals who claim membership in racialized communities. I'm suggesting that we need a new age—with a new agenda— that directly addresses the structural racism that determines who goes to prison and who does not, who attends university and who does not, who has health insurance and who does not. The old agenda facilitates assaults on affirmative action, as Ward Connerly pointed out in his campaign for Proposition 209 in California. From his vantage point, what is most important today is the protection of the civil rights of white men.

Right. But very smart strategies are being used, ones that displace attention from issues of racial justice by speaking in terms of multiculturalism. An example is last year's court decision in

Michigan—Grutter v. Bollinger—that says that affirmative action must be administered for the sake of preserving multiculturalism. What is the difference between multiculturalism and racial justice?

There's a huge difference. Diversity is one of those words in the contemporary lexicon that presumes to be synonymous with antiracism. Multiculturalism is a category that can admit both progressive and deeply conservative interpretations. There's corporate multiculturalism because corporations have discovered that it is more profitable to create a diverse work place.

Benetton multiculturalism.

Yes. They have discovered that blacks and Latinos and Asians are willing to work as hard, or even harder, than their white counterparts. But this means that we should embrace a strong politically inflected multiculturalism, which emphasizes cross-racial community and continued struggles for equality and justice. That is to say cross-racial community not for the purpose of creating a beautiful "bouquet of flowers" or an enticing "bowl of salad"—which are some of the metaphorical representations of multiculturalism—but as a way of challenging structural inequalities and fighting for justice. This version of multiculturalism has radical potential.

And along with the question of multiculturalism and racial jus-
tice, there's another question that tremendously worries me per-
sonally, existentially. That is, we keep talking about the
"browning" of the United States; that by the year 2050 a quar-
ter of the American population will be of Latino descent. Do you
think that this browning of America will entail an eclipse of the
quest for racial justice?

Why should it?

Conservatives claim that questions of racial justice are essentially
black questions . . . and that multiculturalism and racial inte-
gration of Latinos are separate from racial justice work, affir-
mative action or reparations.

Well, you see, that's the problem, and it seems to me that
contemporary ideologies encourage this assumption that
racial competition and conflict are the only possible relationships across communities of people of color. It is as if these
communities are always separate and never intersect. But, if
one looks at the labor movement, for example, there are
numerous historical examples of Black-Latino solidarity and
alliances. Regardless of which community might be numer-
ically larger, without such solidarities and alliances, there can
be no hope for an anti-racist future. At the same time, it is
important to acknowledge that this is a new era. Conditions
of postcoloniality here in the United States and throughout

the world convey the message that the "West" has been forever changed. Europe is not what it used to be. It is no longer
defined by its whiteness. The same thing, of course, is true in
the U.S. among black people who are used to being the
"superior minority." We must let go of this claim. There is
this prevalent idea that because black people established the
historical anti-racist agenda for the United States of America, they will always remain its most passionate advocates.
But black people as a collective cannot live on the laurels of
its historical past. We have recently received harsh lessons
about conservative possibilities in black communities.
"Black" can not simply be considered an uncontestable syn-
onym of progressive politics. The work of progressive activists
is to build opposition to conservatism—regardless of the
racial background of its proponents. That black and Latino
communities cannot find common cause is one example of
this conservatism. Our job today is to promote cross-racial
communities of struggle that arise out of common—and
hopefully radical—political aspirations.

*In the early 1970s Nixon and Hoover called you an enemy of the
State. They also called you a terrorist. Yet, you produced a major
indictment of the prison at the time—your autobiography. For
the past 30 years since then your work has continued to gravitate
around prisons. Are there differences between the emphasis of
your writing in the 1970s and that of work that you have
recently published, for instance,* Are Prisons Obsolete?

Well, I guess you are right—a protracted engagement with the prison system has literally defined my life. My interest in these issues actually precedes my own imprisonment. I grew up with stories of Sacco and Vanzetti, the Scottsboro Nine, and later Nelson Mandela, and before I was arrested I had been active in a number of campaigns to free political prisoners. What I have been trying to do recently is to think critically about the lasting contributions of that period and to take seriously the work of prison intellectuals. I have also been trying to think more systematically about the ways in which slavery continues to live on in contemporary institutions—as in the cases of the death penalty and the prison, for example.

Let me try to back up and summarize this very long trajectory. My first encounter with the prison as a focus of activism and reflection was staged by my participation in various campaigns to free political prisoners during my teenage years. During the height of my vocation as an activist, I focused very sharply on organizing campaigns to free political prisoners arrested in the late sixties and early seventies. My own imprisonment was a consequence of this work. While I was in jail, I began to think—at least superficially—about the possibility of an analysis that shifted its emphasis to the institution of the prison, not only as an apparatus to repress political activists, but also as an institution deeply connected to the maintenance of racism. For this approach, I was deeply indebted to George Jackson. Now I am trying to think about the ways that the prison reproduces forms of racism based on the traces of slavery that can still be discovered within the contemporary criminal justice system. There is, I believe, a clear relationship between the rise of the prison-industrial-complex in the era of global capitalism and the persistence of structures in the punishment system that originated with slavery. I argue, for example, that the most compelling explanation for the routine continuation of capital punishment in the U.S.—which, in this respect, is alone among industrialized countries in the world—is the racism that links the death penalty to slavery. One implication of such an analysis is that we need to think differently about the workings of contemporary structural racism—which can injure white people as well as people of color, who are, of course, its main targets. Another implication is that we can think differently about reparations. One of the major priorities of the reparations movement should be the abolition of the death penalty.

The prison in the United States has become a kind of ghetto. And if I hear you correctly, you're suggesting that in the United States there cannot be a non-racial prison system—that a non-racist prison system would be an oxymoron.

Yes, I suppose you may put it that way. As a matter of fact, there is an assumption that an institution of repression, if it does its work equitably—if it treats, say, white people in the same way it treats black people—is an indication of progress under the sign of equality and justice. I am very suspicious of such an abstract approach. James Byrd was lynched in Jasper, Texas a few years ago by a group of white supremacists. . . . Do you remember that incident?

Yes, and he was dragged around as well.

Two of the white men who helped to carry out the lynching were sentenced to death. That moment was celebrated as a victory, as if the cause of racial justice is served by meting out the same horrendous and barbaric treatment to white people that black people have historically suffered. That kind of equality does not make a great deal sense to me.

Can you expand on that? In other words, there's a continuum between the antebellum period, the reconstruction, the ghettos, and the death penalty, which are equally racialized. Indeed, all of these institutions and spaces seem to have their roots in slavery. Are these links and continuities what you are alluding to?

What is interesting is that slavery as an institution, during the end of the eighteenth century and throughout the ninetenth century, for example, managed to become a receptacle for all of those forms of punishment that were considered to be barbaric by the developing democracy. So rather than abolish the death penalty outright, it was offered refuge within slave law.

This meant that white people eventually were released from the threat of death for most offenses, with murder remaining as the usual offense leading to a white's execution. Black slaves, on the other hand, were subject to the death penalty in some states for as many as seventy different offenses. One might say that the institution of slavery served as a receptacle for those forms of punishment considered to be too uncivilized to be inflicted on white citizens within a democratic society. With the abolition of slavery this clearly racialized form of punishment became de-racialized and persists today under the guise of color-blind justice. Capital punishment continues to be inflicted disproportionately on black people, but when the black person is sentenced to death, he/she comes under the authority of law as the abstract juridical subject, as a rights-bearing individual, not as a member of a racialized community that has been subjected to conditions that make him/her a prime candidate for legal repression. Thus the racism becomes invisible and unrecognizable. In this respect, he/she is "equal" to his/her white counterpart, who therefore is not entirely immune to the hidden racism of the law.

The structures of these institutions are thoroughly racialized. An example would be the way in which prisoners get their rights suspended and enter a type of civil death. This is also part of this racism, right? You mention in your book Are Prisons Obsolete? *that Bush would not have been elected if prisoners had been allowed to vote.*

Absolutely. What I find interesting is that disenfranchisement of prisoners is most often assumed to have a self-evident logic. Most people in this country do not question the process that robs prisoners—and in many states former felons—of their right to vote. They might find it amusing to discover that a few states still allow prisoners to vote. Why has the disenfranchisement of people convincted of felonies become so much a part of the common sense thought structures of people in this country? I believe that this also has its roots in slavery. A white contemporary of slavery might have remarked: "Of course slaves weren't supposed to vote. They weren't full citizens." In the same way people think today, "Of course prisoners aren't supposed to vote. They aren't really citizens any more. They are in prison." There remains a great deal of work to do if we wish to transform these popular attitudes.

Your recent work also mentions that there is a symbiotic relationship between the prison-industrial-complex and the military-industrial-complex. How are those relationships sustained? How are they interwoven?

Well, first I should indicate that the use of the term *prison-industrial-complex* by scholars, activists, and others has been strategic, designed precisely to resonate with the term *military-industrial-complex*. When one considers the extent to which both complexes earn profit while producing the means to maim and kill human beings and devour social resources, then the basic structural similarities become apparent. During the Vietnam War, it became obvious that military production was becoming an increasingly more central element of the economy, one that had begun to colonize the economy, so to speak. One can detect similar proclivities in the prison-industrial-complex. It is no longer a minor niche for a few companies; the punishment industry is on the radar of countless numbers of corporations in the manufacturing and service industries. Prisons are identified for their potential as consumers and for their potential cheap labor. There are many ways one might describe the symbiotic relationship of the military and the prison. I will focus on one of the most obvious connections: the striking similarities in the human populations of the two respective institutions. In fact, many young people—especially young people of color—who enlist in the military often do so in order to escape a trajectory of poverty, drugs, and illiteracy that will lead them directly to prison. Finally, a brief observation that has enormous implications: At least one corporation in the defense industry has actively recruited prison labor. Think about this picture: prisoners building weaponry that aids the government in is quest for global dominance.

You have also argued that there is no correlation between crime and imprisonment. That the "prisonization" of American society has transformed the racial landscape of the United States. What is this relationship then? We are under the assumption that

we have so many prisoners because there are so many people com-
mitting crimes, but you argue otherwise.

Well the link that is usually assumed in popular and scholarly
discourse is that crime produces punishment. What I have
tried to do—together with many other public intellectuals,
activists, scholars—is to encourage people to think about the
possibility that punishment may be a consequence of other
forces and not an inevitable consequence of the commission
of crime. Which is not to say that people in prisons have not
committed what we call "crimes" I'm not making that argument at all. Regardless of who has or has not committed
crimes, punishment, in brief, can be seen more as a conse
quence of racialized surveillance. Increased punishment is
most often a result of increased surveillance. Those communities that are subject to police surveillance are much more
likely to produce more bodies for the punishment industry.
But even more important, imprisonment is the punitive solution to a whole range of social problems that are not being
addressed by those social institutions that might help people
lead better, more satisfying lives. This is the logic of what has
been called the imprisonment binge: Instead of building
housing, throw the homeless in prison. Instead of developing
the educational system, throw the illiterate in prison. Throw
people in prison who lose jobs as the result of de-industrial-
ization, globalization of capital, and the dismantling of the welfare state. Get rid of all of them. Remove these dispensable

populations from society. According to this logic the prison becomes a way of disappearing people in the false hope of disappearing the underlying social problems they represent.

Is this also—this process of disappearing people without resolving the social contradictions—related to the 1996 Welfare Reform Act and the subsequent increase in the number of women in prison?

Absolutely. As a matter of fact, women still constitute the fastest growing sector of the imprisoned population— although immigrants may not be far behind—not only here but in other parts of the world as well. In part, this has to do with the disestablishment of the welfare system, which, although it did not provide a serious solution to the problems of single, unemployed, or low-skilled mothers, was nevertheless a safety net. One visits a women's prison and sees the huge number of women imprisoned in connection with drug-related charges, and it should not be difficult to see the awful consequences of dismantling even the most inadequate alternatives, such as the federal program Aid to Dependent Children.

Do you think, in parallel to the symbiotic relationship that exists between the military-industrial and the prison-industrial complexes, that there's a symbiotic relationship between the prison industry and the judiciary in the United States?

Well, but they are part of the same system: law, law enforcement and punishment. The sentencing practices that have developed over the last two decades are immediately responsible for the huge number of people that are behind bars. The more than two million people in the various jails and prisons are there as an appalling consequence of mandatory sentencing laws, "truth in sentencing," three strikes, etc.

There's a fascinating phenomenon—one that you talk about in your work—that at the same time that building more prisons seems to make people feel safer, that there has actually been a declining rate of crime since the 1970s. Why is that? Why do people feel safer having prisons?

You are correct to ask what makes people *feel* safer, rather than what actually makes people be safer. It is ironic that with the continued pandemic of intimate violence—violence in the home—that the family is still considered to be a safe place, a haven. The threat to security appears always to come from the outside, from the imagined external enemy. There are multiple figurations of the enemy (including the immigrant and the terrorist), but the prisoner, imagined as murderer and rapist, looms large as a menace to security. So now there are over *two million* people behind bars, the majority of whom have not been convicted of violent crimes, considered to be embodiments of the enemy. This is supposed to make people feel better, but what it really does is divert their attention away from those threats to security that come from the military, police, profit-seeking corporations, and sometimes from one's own intimate partners.

Today people seem to feel that we are continually under the threat of a possible crime, a sense that seems to be instigated by the media. Is this sense of panic fabricated, or is there some substance to it?

Well, these moral panics have always erupted at particular conjunctures. We can think about the moral panic about black rapists, particularly in the aftermath of slavery. The myth of the black rapist was a key component of an ideological strategy designed to recast the problems of managing newly freed black people in the aftermath of slavery. And so the moral panic around crime is not related to a rise in crime in any material sense. Rather, it is related to the problem of managing large populations— particularly people of color— who have been rendered dispensable by the system of global capitalism. This may be a superficial analogy but I do think it works.

In this complex web of relations between criminalizing populations, punishment, and prisonization, you make a suggestion that is quite glaring to me, and very provocative. You say that the criminalization of youth because of the so-called "war on drugs" occurred simultaneously with an explosion in the use of doctor-

prescribed psychotropic drugs. But there's a difference between crack and Prozac, isn't there?

Well, yes. One provides enormous amount of profit for the pharmaceutical corporations and the other doesn't—although street drugs do provide enormous profit for underground drug economies. While I would hesitate to talk about the chemical similarities or dissimilarities, I would argue that there is a major contradiction between the "war on drugs" discourse and the corporate discourse within which legal psychotropic drugs, available by prescription to those who have money or health insurance, and are promoted by the pharmaceuticals as chemical inducements to relaxation, happiness, productivity, etc.

Ritalin for the kids . . . and Viagra for the older folks, for instance.

That's right. It seems that there is a drug prescription available for any possible problem one might have. How might you feel if you were a poor person at the receiving end of the daily barrage of commercials about the miraculous powers of drugs available by prescription? This commercial discourse must help create an increase drug traffic—both the legal and the underground kinds.

In your work you have also discussed the continuum connecting the Cold War with the war on drugs to the current war on ter-

rorism. What are the continuums, the similarities? What are the differences?

Well. It would be very complicated to explore all of the differences and similarities, but I would like to suggest that the terrain for the production of the terrorist as a figure in the American imaginary reflects vestiges of previous moral panics as well, including those instigated by the mass fear of the criminal and the communist. Willie Horton is the most dramatic example of the former. Anti-communism successfully mobilized national—perhaps I should say nationalist—anxieties, as does the so-called war on terrorism today. None of these figures are entirely new, although the emphasis has been different at different historical conjunctures.

Perhaps I can be allowed to draw an example from my own life. When I was on the FBI's Ten Most Wanted list, President Nixon publicly referred to me as a terrorist. In this case all three figures were articulated together: I was communist, terrorist, and criminal. Collective emotional responses to the evocation of the terrorist are entangled with those summoned by the criminal and the communist. All represent an external enemy against which the nation mobilizes in order to save itself. Nationalism always requires an enemy—whether inside or outside the nation. This is not really new. The material consequences are of course horrendous. People of Muslim or Arab descent—or those who appear to be Muslim or Arab (whatever that might mean) are suffering terribly inside the U.S. and European countries. The U.S. occupation of Iraq and Afghanistan is producing dreadful and unimaginable consequences.

You have been working on a major new book entitled Prisons and History. *Can you tell us about it?*

O.K. Hopefully it will encourage people to think not only about the institution of the prison but also about the particular version of democracy to which we are asked to consent. Democratic rights and liberties are defined in relation to what is denied to people in prison. So we might ask, what kind of democracy do we currently inhabit? The kind of democracy that can only invent and develop itself as the affirmative face of the horrors depicted in the Abu Ghraib photographs, the physical and mental agonies produced on a daily basis in prisons here and all over the world. This is a flawed conception of democracy.

I want to touch on an example that challenges conventional ideas about the separation of prison and society, one that resituates our shocked responses to the recent images of sexual coercion in Iraq. We acknowledge the fact that women in prisons all over the world are forced, on a regular basis, to undergo strip searches and cavity searches. That is to say their vaginas and rectums are searched. Any woman capable of imagining herself—not the other, but rather herself—searched in such a manner will inexorably experience it as sexual assault. But since it occurs in prison, society assumes that this kind of assault is a normal and routine aspect of women's imprisonment and is self-justified by the mere fact of imprisonment. Society assumes that this is what happens when a woman goes to prison. That this is what happens to the citizen who is divested of her citizenship rights and that it is therefore right that the prisoner be subjected to sexual coercion.

I want to urge people to think more deeply about the very powerful and profound extent to which such practices inform the kind of democracy we inhabit today. I would like to urge people to think about different versions of democracy, future democracies, democracies grounded in socialism, democracies in which those social problems that have enabled the emergence of the prison-industrial-complex will be, if not completely solved, at least encountered and acknowledged.

Sexual Coercion, Prisons, and Feminist Responses

Let's begin with the disclosures that the U.S. has been torturing people as part of its war on terror—not only in Guantánamo Bay but also in Iraq, Afghanistan, and by way of the countries to which the U.S. ships detainees to be interrogated. What is your take on this?

A lot of information is being made public about the abuses committed by the U.S.—the torture, abuse, the sexual violation of people detained at the notorious Abu Ghraib prison in Baghdad, and elsewhere. As difficult as it is to view the photographs of torture taken at Abu Ghraib, as horrendous as they may appear—particularly to people in this country who find it hard to believe that a young white woman from North Carolina could be an active perpetrator of the tortures portrayed—these abusive practices cannot be dismissed as anomalies. They emanate from techniques of punishment deeply embedded in the history of the institution of prison. While I know that it may be difficult for many people to accept the fact that similar forms of repression can be discovered inside U.S. domestic prisons, it is important not to fixate on these tortures as freakish irregularities. How do we pose questions about the violence associated with the importation of U.S.-style democracy to Iraq? What kind of democracy is willing to treat human beings as refuse? I think we know the answer to this question.

"A picture is worth a thousand words," goes the popular saying. In the case of Abu Ghraib, however, the pictures seem to be both expressive and repressive. The fixation on the pictures seems to suggest that what is horrible is that the pictures and videos *exist and not that* torture *exists. Should we not be more horrified that if these pictures had not been leaked, we would never have had the scandal necessary to confront the U.S. practice of torture?*

What is perhaps even more horrible is that we project so much onto the ostensible power of the image that what it represents, what it depicts, loses its force. The philosopher Theodor Adorno wrote at length about the unrepresentability of the most brutal human acts, such as those committed by the Third Reich. We might also reflect on the unrepresentability of slavery and its myriad violences, and on the unrepresentability of torture in U.S. military prisons. The images depicting torture at Abu Ghraib were released into an environment so charged with assumptions about the hegemony of U.S. democracy that the images themselves were overwhelmingly understood in the context of the need to explain them in relation to democracy. In other words, how could we understand the images as depicting acts that fundamentally contradicted dominant assumptions about U.S. democracy?

The concern with rescuing U.S. democracy pushed the suffering of the prisoners into the background. It seems to me that the widespread expressions of shock and revulsion in relation to the photographs asked, "how this is possible?" "how can this happen?" and asserted, "this is not supposed to happen." There was disbelief and an impulse toward justification, rather than an engagement with the contemporary meaning of torture and violence.

Images are very complicated and we haven't promoted, at least not in a mass sense, a visual literacy necessary to critically understand them. To think of the image as an unmediated representation is problematic and often has the effect of producing precisely the opposite of what was expected. I'm thinking of the Rodney King controversy. For example, we saw the police beating Rodney King on video, but the prosecutor was able to develop a particular interpretation of that image that bolstered his claim that Rodney King was the aggressor. So I think it is important not to assume that the image has a self-evident relationship to its object. And it is important to consider the particular economy within which images are produced and consumed.

The photographs enter into an economy that seems to say, "you see, we can show this because we are a democracy," and in the process the fact that the same democracy committed the act of tor-

ture is effaced. I guess this is what happened with Rodney King as well. Can you elaborate?

We might talk about the particular interpretive communities within which the images were released. Of course, the dominant responses implicated specific individuals as the perpetrators of the atrocities represented in the photographs, implying that they should not be interpreted as a general comment on the state of U.S. democracy. In other words, these acts of torture and sexual coercion are only conceivable as the work of aberrant individuals. So this interpretive framework helped to constitute the particular economy in which the images circulated. Of course, in some of the alternative media there were more complicated interpretations proposed, but the dominant media proceeded as if the answers to the questions posed by the photographs were already known.

Several people have compared the Abu Ghraib images to lynching pictures from the turn of the century. Is it proper to compare them, despite some radical differences? After all, the lynching pictures were of public events in which citizens killed fellow citizens in rites of racial purity, with local authorities often sanctioning them. The Abu Ghraib pictures, on the other hand, are of soldiers torturing so-called enemy combatants, if not following explicit commands, at least performing their soldierly duty. There is also a pornographic staging in the Abu Ghraib photographs that is absent, in my view, from lynching pictures.

Since you raise the question, I do think that there is a connection between these two sets of photographic images and I think it is important to recognize their kinship across historical eras and geopolitical locales. First of all, let me answer your question about citizens killing citizens. Lynchings could be photographed as celebratory gatherings precisely because those who participated assumed that they were destroying others who could not possibly be included in the community of citizens. One could argue that lynching precisely defined its victims as beyond the possibility of citizenship. Even though the victims formally may have been citizens— second-class citizens at best—lynching was one of the ways in which the impossibility of equal citizenship was reinforced, especially when you consider the relationship between lynching and the legal apparatus. Lynching was extra-legal, but it was linked very closely to the state's machinery of justice. Although the participants were not direct representatives of the state in carrying out these lynchings, they considered themselves to be doing the work of the state.

In the South during the post-Civil War era, lynchings played a major role in establishing an environment conducive to the transformation of state constitutions so as to subordinate the legal apparatus to the requirements of racism. Lynchings facilitated the consolidation of Jim Crow. But lynchings also helped to validate capital punishment, which had been debated since the revolutionary period. I see the death penalty and lynching as very closely linked, particularly when one considers that they both have their origins in slavery and that communally inflicted death was—and still is—much more likely to be justified when the dead person's body is black than when it is white. At the same time, we should keep in mind that when such processes become institutionalized, white bodies can also bear the brunt of this racist violence.

The black targets of lynching—construed as representatives of a racialized population—can be seen as individual victims in the construction of a collective racial enemy. This was the important ideological work of lynching. The lynching victim becomes an individual materialization of an ideological enemy. In that sense I think that there are clear parallels between acts of lynching and the events at Abu Ghraib despite the different socio-historical circumstances. Lynching was public; today torture is hidden behind prison walls. Of course punishment has moved historically from public spectacle to more hidden forms of violence, especially with the creation of the prison. Military prisons, as they currently exist, incorporate the regimes and practices developed within the domestic prison system. As the dominance of imprisonment increased and lynching waned under the impact, the public dimension of imprisonment began to give way to hidden forms of violence.

Today, even legal executions are concealed. Both military and domestic prisons carry the mandate to hide the real nature of punishment from all except its perpetrators and its targets. The contemporary representability of execution is possible only insofar as it appears to have abandoned all its previous violence. Lethal injection is represented as swift, humane and painless. The irony, of course, is that the concealment of punishment has enabled the proliferation of the worst forms of brutality and violence.

In answer to your question regarding the pornographic dimension of the Abu Ghraib photographs, I would have to argue that there was also a very explicit pornographic dimension to the photographs of lynching. First, consider the ideological environment and the dominant explanation proposed by the advocates (as well as some opponents) of lynching: black men were supposed to be inclined to rape white women. The lynchings themselves were frequently accompanied by sexual violence and sexual mutilation, castration, dismemberment, as well as the sale of body parts as lynching artefacts. Photographs of lynchings, produced as postcards—historical counterparts to amusement park postcards today—were clearly pornographic. This captures what is perhaps the best definition of pornography: objectification of the body, the privileging of the dismembered body. I would have to think about this a bit further, but I think that there is a very revealing parallel between the sexual coercion and sexual violence within the Abu Ghraib context and the role sexual violence plays in lynching.

Orlando Patterson has suggested that lynchings were part of a blood rite, a type of racial cleansing.[11] *I mention this because I would like to ask whether what we have in the Abu Ghraib pictures is a new racial contract?*

A new racial contract in what sense?

In the sense of whites against Islamic "others," where religion is treated racially. A new racial contract in which "Americans" are unified against this "other," this new enemy.

I'm reluctant to work with the assumption that the anti-black racial contract is primary in all respects. Here in the U.S., we have learned to speak about race in terms that emanated from the struggle for black equality. And although the hegemonic struggle against racism has definitely been a contestation with anti-black racism, throughout the history of this country, there have been other racialized histories and other forms of racial domination, not the least of which is the genocidal assault on indigenous populations. I think it is extremely important to acknowledge the mutability of race and the alterability of the structures of racism. This is especially important because there is often times a tendency to work with hierarchies of racism. I refer frequently to Elizabeth Martinez's notion of an "oppression Olympics": who is the most oppressed? She argues, of course, that to pursue the question is a losing game in every respect.

So, yes, I think it is important to acknowledge the extent to which racism today is fueled by the "war on terror." It is a very complicated process of racialization because it allegedly targets people of Middle Eastern descent, but that, even as a geopolitical category, is suspect. Bush's war against terror exploits religion and thus targets communities around the world that practice Islam—especially in South and Southeast Asia, using the justification offered by Huntington in his "clash of civilizations" thesis.

When we consider the way the conventional weapons of racism have been redeployed, along with new ones—the USA PATRIOT Act, the proliferation of detention centers and military prisons—we might argue that as horrendous as this explosion of violence may be, it contains important lessons about the nature of racism. These contemporary lessons are more clearly apprehended than those associated with the racism we recognize as embedded in the history of black people in this country. But it is difficult to ask people to acknowledge the obsolescence of historical racism, because we have an affective attachment to the identities that are based on that history. Nevertheless, the varities of racism that define our present era are so deeply embedded in institutional structures and so complexly mediated that they now appear to be detached from the persons they harm with their violence.

The Bush administration has insisted that the global "war on terror" is not a crusade, not religious war. Yet, there have been some recent disclosures, in particular in a book by Erik Saar, a veteran of Guantánamo, that makes it clear that the U.S. has, at Guantánamo and Abu Ghraib, been using torture techniques specifically designed to violate the detainees' cultural and religious values. He describes, for example, women interrogators using sexually explicit or S&M clothing, pretending to touch prisoners with menstrual blood and then withholding water so that they the detainee cannot clean themself.[12] *They are using Islamic culture as a weapon, using a person's Islamic culture as a sensibility that can be tortured. Here we have a form of religious war, but in this case waged by the West.*

First of all, I would say that I am always suspicious when culture is deployed as a strategy or an answer, because culture is so much more complicated. The apparent cultural explanation of these forms of torture reveals a very trivial notion of culture. Why is it assumed that a non-Muslim man approached by a female interrogator dressed as a dominatrix, attempting to smear menstrual blood on him, would react any differently from a Muslim man? These assumptions about culture are themselves racist.

When critics of the tortures carried out under the auspices of the Bush administration cavalierly assume that the tortures are simply exploiting the fact that Islamic culture is inherently more sexist than what we call western culture, the critics themselves participate in this violence. These misunderstandings of culture are thus very effective as weapons in the war against terror.

Culture is not static, it is alive; it is about everyday practices, it is about change, it is about difference. The assumption that one can know all that is important to know about an individual—a prisoner incarcerated at Abu Ghraib or Guantánamo, for example—if one knows her or his "culture," is itself a racist proposition. It is an indication of the extent to which the U.S. conducts the war on terror, the war for global dominance, with any available weapons. Ideological weapons are often times the most powerful. The notion of culture promoted by the warriors on terror is predicated on the idea that there must be a hierarchy of cultures within which "Islamic culture" is already inferior. To explain the tortures within this pseudo-cultural framework is to define the people who are being tortured as already inferior. So I wonder whether it might be possible to think about your question in a different way—in a way that is critical of what is actually being done to these human beings, to the bodies of the Iraqi prisoners, and in a way that understands that U.S. interrogation methods comment more on U.S. strategies and methods than on the people who are suffer the torture.

So you are suggesting that we see the actions deployed by the torturers as not representing cultural understanding of Arab and Middle Eastern peoples, but only the prejudices of the torturers?

Yes, exactly. You see, what happens is that we may think that we're challenging Huntington's "clash of civilizations" thesis, but we're using the same terms, the same frame. The assumption of cultural inferiority remains. And, in the final analysis, the uncritical acceptance of certain cultural terms works as much to our disadvantage as the arguments justifying torture that we attempt to refute.

This is analogous to what you said earlier with respect to the images from Abu Ghraib: how they enter into an economy, but become eviscerated or pre-empted, how images are communicated within an interpretative frame that makes it easy to buy into the implicit assumption that a person might deserve torture simply because of their particular culture.

Yes, and even if we are morally opposed to torture, even if we think we are passionately opposed to torture, the very process of taking on an oppositional position that draws on the terms of racism militates against the possibility of equality or solidarity. We end up reinforcing the inferiority of the person who is the victim of torture. It is a kind of epistemic violence that coincides with or accompanies the physical violence we think we are contesting. Anti-Arab racism has rendered it very difficult to acknowledge the leadership of those communities that suffered torture in Iraq. The victims of torture have been objectified as a problem liberal U.S. citizens must seek to solve. In many ways, this recapitulates the vexed history of struggles against anti-black racism within the United States. Drastic moves were required—the expulsion of white members of SNCC, for example—to reveal the dynamic of racism and what has been called unacknowledged white privilege within movement circles. This is not to say that every white civil rights activist was openly racist, but rather to insist on the power—then and now—of ideologies of racial inferiority.

In The Torture Papers: The Road to Abu Ghraib,[13] *we are confronted with the naked truth that our government consciously and deliberately violated one of the most fundamental rights in international humanitarian law, the prohibition against torture. But it seems that we are being blackmailed: either we talk about torture or we don't, and if we do, the issue focuses around what kinds of torture are acceptable and which are not.*

Yes, that is the trap, but it seems to me that we have no choice but to discuss it. But we must ask what larger issues frame the questions we are allowed to ask about torture. As you said, those questions are fairly constrained: does this constitute torture or does it not constitute torture? So how can we break out of that frame, moving beyond the question of what is and what is not torture? Some of the official memos pointed toward utterly ridiculous conversations about how not to label particular forms of violence, such as sleep deprivation, standing for long periods of time, etc., as torture. They pointed to overt efforts to evade accepted international definitions of torture and even attempts to evade U.S. legal frameworks. The memos also reveal an effort to render routine and mundane what might otherwise be defined as torture.

We tend to think about torture as an aberrant event. Torture is extraordinary and can be clearly distinguished from other regimes of punishment. But if we consider the various forms of violence linked to the practice of imprisonment—circuits of violence linked to one another—then we begin to see that the extraordinary has some connection to the ordinary. Within the radical movement in defense of women prisoners' rights, the routine strip and cavity search is recognized as a form of sexual assault. As activists like Debbie Kilroy of Sisters Inside[14] have pointed out, if uniforms are replaced with civilian clothes—the guard's and the prisoner's—then the act of strip searching would look exactly like the sexual violence that is experienced by the prisoner who is ordered to remove her clothing, stoop, and spread her buttocks. In the case of vaginal and rectal searches, routinely performed on women prisoners in the U.S., this continuum of sexual violence is even more obvious.

To break free of this blackmail, as you put it, to move beyond the permissible terms, it might be helpful to consider the connections between everyday prison violence and torture. Of course, we know that some of the military personnel involved in the Abu Ghraib scandal had previously served as prison guards in domestic prisons. This points to a deeper connection between the situation at Abu Ghraib and domestic imprisonment practices. It is not a coincidence that Charles Graner, recently tried and convicted for his role in the tortures, had been employed as prison guard at SCI-Greene, the facility where death row prisoners—including Mumia Abu Jamal—are housed in Pennsylvania. As a matter of fact there were at least two lawsuits filed against him for abuse within that prison. Of course I don't want to suggest that Graner's previous history as a prison guard is a sufficient explanation for the tortures at Abu Ghraib, especially if such an argument is used to absolve the military hierarchy and the Bush government of responsibility. Rather I am attempting to highlight the links between the institution of the military prison and that of the domestic prison. What is routinely accepted as necessary conduct by prison guards can easily turn into the kind of torture that violates international standards, especially under the impact of racism. Fanon once made the point that violence is always there on the horizon of racism. Rather than rely on a taxonomy of those acts that are defined as torture and those that are not, it may be more revealing to examine how one set of institutionalized practices actually enables the other.

Let me return to the question of the racial contract we were talking about earlier. Implicit in that question was another, namely, whether this use of torture has given expression to a new contract: the equal opportunity, racial-sexual torture contract in which gender equality means that all can participate equally in degrading themselves as they inflict suffering on prisoners. There is a very explicit gender dimension to the Abu Ghraib pictures . . .

The representations of women soldiers were quite dramatic and most people found them utterly shocking. But we might also say that they provided powerful evidence of what the most interesting feminist analyses have tried to explain: that there is a difference between the body gendered as female and the set of discourses and ideologies that inform the sex/gender system. These images were a kind of visualization of this sex/gender conjunction. We are not accustomed to visually apprehending the difference between female bodies and male supremacist ideologies. Therefore seeing images of a woman engaged in behavior that we associate with male dominance is startling. But it should not be, especially if we take seriously what we know about the social construction of gender. Especially within institutions that rely on ideologies of male dominance, women can be easily mobilized to commit the same acts of violence expected of men—just as black people, by virtue of being black, are not therefore immune from the charge of promoting racism.

The images to which you're referring to evoke a memory of a comment made by Colin Powell during the first Gulf war. He said that the military was the most democratic institution in our society and created a framework in which people could escape the constraints of race and, we can add today, gender as well. This notion of the military as a levelling institution, one that constitutes each member as equal, is frightening and dangerous, because you must eventually arrive at the conclusion that this equality is about equal opportunity to kill, to torture, to engage in sexual coercion. At the time I found it very bizarre that Powell would point to the most hierarchal institution, with its rigid chain of command, as the epitome of democracy. Today, I would say that such a conception of democracy reveals the problems and limitations of civil rights strategies and discourses.

This is true not only with respect to race and gender, but with respect to sexuality as well. Why is the effort to challenge sexism and homophobia in the military largely defined by the question of admission to existing hierarchies and not also a powerful critique of the institution itself? Equality might be considered to be the equal right to refuse and resist.

This is how I would rephrase your original question: How might we consider the visual representation of female bodies collaborating in acts of sexual torture—forcing Arab men to engage in public masturbation, for example—as calling for a feminist analysis that challenges prevailing assumptions that the only possible relationship between women and violence requires women to be the victims?

You've anticipated my next question. Barbara Ehrenreich has written that a "certain kind of feminist naiveté died at Abu Ghraib. It was a feminism that saw men as the perpetual perpetrators, women as the perpetual victims, and male sexual violence against women as the root of all injustice."[15] What do Guantánamo and Abu Ghraib mean to feminists?

To naïve feminists? Here I would have to place emphasis on "naïve." Of course this question of what counts as feminism has been hotly debated for who knows how long. Nevertheless I think that most contemporary feminist theorists and activists acknowledge that the category "woman" is a false universal, thanks largely to the scholarship and activism associated with "women of color feminism." It is true that in popular discourse we have a tendency to use essentialist notions about what women do or do not and what men do or do not. Still, the notion that men are naturally inclined to commit sexual violence and that this is the root of all injustice is something that most good feminists gave up a long time ago. I'm not sure why Barbara Ehrenreich would formulate a response to the Abu Ghraib photographs in this way. A more productive approach would be to think more precisely about forms of socialization and institutionalization and about the extent to which these misogynist strategies and modes of violence are available to women as well as men. When one looks at certain practices often unquestionably accepted by women guards in U.S. prisons, one can glimpse the potential for the sexual coercion that was at the core of the torture strategies at Abu Ghraib. I return, therefore, to the question of those established circuits of violence in which both women and men participate, the techniques of racism administered not only by white people, but by black, Latino, Native American, and Asian people as well. Today we might say that we have all been offered an equal opportunity to perpetuate male dominance and racism.

*So you would rather put the emphasis on the institutions of vio-
lence, the institutionalization of certain mechanisms of violence,
rather than on whether it is perpetrated by males or females.*

Exactly. I am referring to a feminist analysis that enables us to
think about these different and sometimes disparate objects and
processes together. Such a feminist approach would not always
be compelled to engage centrally with "women" or even "gender," but when it does attempt to understand gender, it pays
special attention to the production of gender in and through
such institutions. More generally, I would say that the radical
impulse of feminist analysis is precisely to think disparate
about categories together, to think across disciplinary borders,
to think across categorical divisions. This is precisely what the
Abu Ghraib photographs demand.

*Let me turn the question around and ask you, in light of Abu
Ghraib and Guantánamo, what do U.S. and Western feminists
have to say to Islamic and Middle Eastern women?*

You know, when you asked that question, this historical
image came to mind: white, American feminists traveling to
Iran after the 1979 overthrow of the Shah in an attempt to
educate Iranian women on how best to initiate a feminist trajectory. Or, in contemporary terms, I think about George
and Laura Bush, posing as the liberators of women, explain-
ing that this was one of the motivations for invading

Afghanistan. If the global war against terror is justified with ideas about the superiority of U.S. democracy, it is equally dangerous to assume that U.S. feminism—whether liberal or radical—is superior to the feminisms in other parts of the world. Perhaps I would repose your question: What do women in those areas of the world that suffer most under Bush's policy of global war have to say to western feminists? It seems to me that those of us here in the U.S. who are interested in a transnational feminists project would better serve the cause of freedom by asking questions rather than making proposals. So I would want to know how feminist and working class activists in countries such as Iraq might envision the most productive role for us. In the meantime, we must continue to strengthen the anti-war movement.

You're calling into question the paternalistic assumption in my question, that feminists in the West, and the U.S., have to school Islamic women about how to proceed. They can do that work themselves.

Exactly. We have not yet moved beyond the assumption that the most advanced feminists in the world—whether they are white or people of color—reside in the U.S. or in Europe. This is a form of racism that forecloses the possibility of solidarity.

In your work on prisons you have noted that sexual coercion is fundamental to prison regimes. The Guantánamo and Abu Ghraib sexual torture revelations, however, are implanting the idea that such extremes only occur offshore and are rare occurrences. It is as though the prison-industrial system had duplicated itself outside the States in order to divert attention from the everyday domestic reality of torture and sexual coercion.

The prison-industrial-complex embraces a vast set of institutions from the obvious ones, such as the prisons and the various places of incarceration such as jails, "jails in Indian country," immigrant detention centers, and military prisons to corporations that profit from prison labor or from the sale of products that enable imprisonment, media, other government agencies, etc. Ideologies play a central role in consolidating the prison-industrial-complex—for example the marketing of the idea that prisons are necessary to democracy and that they are a major component of the solution of social problems. Throughout the world, racism has become embedded in imprisonment practices: whether in the U.S., Australia, or Europe, you will discover a disproportionate number of people of color and people from the Global South incarcerated in jails and prisons. The everyday tortures experienced by the inhabitants of domestic prisons in the U.S. have enabled the justification of the treatment meted out to prisoners in Abu Ghraib and Guantánamo. As I said earlier, it was hardly accidental that a U.S. prison guard like Charles Graner was recruited to work in Abu Ghraib. He was already familiar with the many ways prison objectifies and dehumanizes its inhabitants.

Yes, this is actually in one of the official reports. It was pointed out that the military actually appointed Graner because of his experience.

Exactly. So the connections do not have to be made from the outside. They are already there to be discovered. As I said before, this is a person whom they must have known had already been the target of at least two lawsuits. In one suit, Graner was accused of throwing a detained man on the floor, kicking and beating him, and placing razorblades in his food. In another lawsuit he was accused of picking up a detainee by the feet and throwing him into a cell.

There is another interesting parallel that I would like to raise in the context of this question, and that is the extent to which the U.S. purposefully transfers detainees to other countries whose governments are free to interrogate and torture them without accountability or restraint. This is process is officially called "extraordinary rendition."

What are the parallels between extraordinary rendition and the trafficking of prisoners across state borders? A number of years ago video footage was made public that depicted the brutal treatment of prisoners in Texas, who were held in a wing of the Brazoria County Detention privately run by Capital Correctional Resources, Inc. This wing held prisoners from Missouri who had been transferred to serve their sentences in Texas. The videotape depicts riot-suppression training strategies and was made available to the media in connection with a lawsuit filed by a prisoner who had been bitten by a dog during the training. Guards kicked prisoners, assaulted them with electric prods, and ordered them to crawl as dogs pursued them. In the aftermath of this violence, Missouri cancelled its contract. But this has not stopped the practice of trafficking the prisoners across state borders, as they are trafficked across national borders.

Of course the practice of extraordinary rendition is designed to enable prisoners to be interrogated and tortured without the U.S. government being held directly accountable. I think that you're right that there is a widespread assumption that torture could never occur within U.S. borders. As a matter of fact, in the earliest conversations about the violation of prisoners' human rights at the military prison in Guantánamo, government officials distinguished between what was allowable offshore and what was allowable within the territory of the United States. They argued that such rights as due process and the right to legal counsel could only be claimed within U.S. borders, but not necessarily outside. Likewise, Alberto Gonzalez characterized the Geneva Conventions as too "quaint" to be applicable to "illegal combatants" incarcerated in Guantánamo Bay.

What are the prospects for prison abolitionism in light of this perpetual war on terror? The prison system, with its surplus violence and torture, seems to have entrenched itself in the Ameri-

can polity. How can we convince Americans that this system is a cancer on the heart of democracy?

There is no straightforward answer to this question, but I can begin to think through some of the implications of your question. The abolitionist movement has a long history, and during various eras, activists have maintained that prevailing conditions in prisons and jails, along with their failure to accomplish their announced purpose, constituted the strongest argument for abolition. Of course, conditions have become even worse over the years and an unimaginable number of people—over two million—are currently held in the network of U.S. prisons and jails. Moreover, we have witnessed how these institutions can be deployed in the U.S. war for global dominance—and this is yet another argument for their abolition.

When we call for prison abolition, we are not imagining the isolated dismantling of the facilities we call prisons and jails. That is not the project of abolition. We proposed the notion of a prison-industrial-complex to reflect the extent to which the prison is deeply structured by economic, social, and political conditions that themselves will also have to be dismantled. So you might say that prison abolition is a way of talking about the pitfalls of the particular version of democracy represented by U.S. capitalism.

Capitalism—especially in its contemporary global form—continues to produce problems that neither it nor its prisons are prepared to solve. So prison abolition requires us to recognize the extent that our present social order—in which are embedded a complex array of social problems—will have to be radically transformed.

Prison abolitionist strategies reflect an understanding of the connections between institutions that we usually think about as disparate and disconnected. They reflect an understanding of the extent to which the overuse of imprisonment is a consequence of eroding educational opportunities, which are further diminished by using imprisonment as a false solution for poor public education. Persisting poverty in the heart of global capitalism leads to larger prison populations, which in turn reinforce the conditions that reproduce poverty.

When I refer to prison abolitionism, I like to draw from the DuBoisian notion of abolition democracy. That is to say, it is not only, or not even primarily, about abolition as a negative process of tearing down, but it is also about building up, about creating new institutions. Although DuBois referred very specifically to slavery and its legal disestablishment as an economic institution, his observation that this negative process by itself was insufficient has deep resonances for prison abolition today. DuBois pointed out that in order to fully abolish the oppressive conditions produced by slavery, new democratic institutions would have to be created. Because this did not occur; black people encountered new forms of slavery—from debt peonage and the convict lease system to segregated and second-class education. The prison system continues to carry out this terrible legacy. It has become a receptacle for all of those human beings who bear the inheritance of the failure to create abolition democracy in the aftermath of slavery. And this inheritance is not only born by black prisoners, but by poor Latino, Native American, Asians, and white prisoners. Moreover, its use as such a receptacle for people who are deemed the detritus of society is on the rise throughout the world.

In light of the global "war on terror," what, then, are the prospects for prison abolitionism? I use the term "prison abolitionism," here, because one of the greatest challenges is to persuade people in all walks of life—but especially those who are most damaged by this institution—that a world without prisons is conceivable. The need to generate a conversation about the prospects for abolition is perhaps even greater now, because linked to the abolition of prisons is the abolition of the instruments of war, the abolition of racism, and, of course, the abolition of the social circumstances that lead poor men and women to look toward the military as their only avenue of escape from poverty, homelessness, and lack of opportunities.

As it was important during the Vietnam War era to locate opposition to that war within a context that acknowledged the expanding military-industrial-complex, so is it now important to reveal the connections between the military-industrial-complex and the prison-industrial-complex and the potential linkages between the forms of resistance that both have provoked. As of now, some 5,500 soldiers are classified as deserters—many of them conscientious objectors. This rising number of resisters within the military reflects the fact that many men and women who have been ordered to Iraq, or fear that they may be ordered, entered the military not with the intention to defend the imperial ambitions of the Bush administration, but rather because they were seeking opportunities for travel, education and other opportunities denied to them because of their racial and class backgrounds. The most well known case is that of Jeremy Hinzman, a young white soldier who unsuccessfully applied for conscientious objector status before being deployed by the Army to Afghanistan, and then later left for Canada when he learned that he was being sent to Iraq. Cindy Sheehan, the Gold Star Mother who spent a month protesting outside of President Bush's Crawford, Texas home while he vacationed their in August 2005, joined the antiwar movement after her son Casey was killed in an ambush in Iraq. Casey, she says, only joined the military to receive financial aid necessary for him to finish college.

Challenges to the military are very much related to the prison abolition struggle. To focus more specifically on prison abolition, I see it as a project that involves re-imagining institutions, ideas, and strategies, and creating new institutions, ideas, and strategies that will render prisons obsolete. That is why I called the book I wrote on prisons, *Are Prisons Obsolete?*[26] It is up to us to insist on the obsolescence of imprisonment as the dominant mode of punishment, but we cannot accomplish this by wielding axes and literally hacking at prison walls, but rather by demanding new democratic institutions that take up the issues that can never be addressed by prisons in productive ways.

Abolition Democracy

Despite the fact that we are legally bound by national and international law not to torture, what the mainstream media seems focused upon debating is whether and when to use torture, as if both national and international law could be suspended if the authorities deem it necessary. How does allowing the public discussion about torture to go on like this entail an attack on the moral integrity of citizens and democracy? Does democracy have anything to do with morality?

The public discussion of torture has been limited by the widespread conviction that democracy is quintessentially American and that any strategy designed to protect or defend the American version of democracy is legitimate. A further problem with this discussion is that the American version of democracy has become increasingly synonymous with capitalism, and capitalism has become progressively more defined by its ability to roam the globe. This is what has framed the conversation about torture and has allowed moral dilemmas about torture to be expressed alongside the notion that permissible forms of violence are necessary if American democracy is to be preserved, both in the U.S. and abroad. In the final analysis, these moral positions against torture do not have the power to challenge American exceptionalism. This unquestioned rift between moral opposition to particular tactics and what is considered to be an imperative to save the nation has enabled a torrent of obfuscating discourse on terrorism on the one hand, and the practice of torture on the other.

Of course, it is important to vigorously object to torture as a technique of control that militates against the ideals and promise of U.S. democracy. But when U.S. democracy becomes the barometer by which any and all political conduct is judged, it is not difficult to transform specific acts of torture into conduct that is tolerable, conduct that does not necessarily violate the community's moral integrity.

There are myriad examples of the inability of morality to transform the sphere of politics. When torture is inflicted on human beings that are marked as racially and culturally inferior—as people from Iraq are—it is not difficult to shift conversations about torture to a more general register, thus ignoring the damage it does to particular individuals.

I am very suspicious of the discourse that implies that torture is more damaging to its perpetrators than to its victims. Yes, it is certainly true that the revelations regarding the brutal techniques of interrogation at Guantánamo and the acts of physical violence and sexual coercion at Abu Ghraib raise significant questions about this society, its government, its military, and its incarceration practices. But when this eclipses the profound suffering of the men and women who have been tortured, it reveals the extent to which the reverberations of morality can support the very racism that enabled the torture in the first place. Thus, it is important not to take for granted that resistance to U.S. torture always implies solidarity with the victims. At the same time that we question the government and military for its role in the perpetration of torture, we must also question our ability to imagine the victims as human beings—individuals—equal in every important respect to those of us who happen to live in the global north.

How, then, can the issue of torture be formulated so as not to authorize a justificatory practice that fails to consider the impact of torture on particular human beings, their bodies and minds? Human rights play a decisive role here—and it is significant that after decades of fraudulently claiming the most progressive human rights record in the world, the United States is now on the defensive. The lawsuits brought by the Center for Constitution Rights on behalf of detainees inside and outside the U.S. are one example of the resistance to the Bush Administration's policies and practices. I have already alluded to the importance of bringing an analysis of racism into the frame. This was clearly lacking in the debates sparked by the release of the Abu Ghraib photographs. How does the meaning of torture shift in accordance with its targets?

Ariel Dorfman once wrote that one of the problems with the discourse of torture in the public sphere is that it puts citizens in the

*position of having to sever themselves from the pain of others.
This is why I call it a crime against moral imagination. We are
being asked as citizens to sever ourselves from the suffering of
others, thus in a way killing the moral and emotive dimensions
of our citizenship.*

In a previous conversation we discussed the framework
within which the images of torture at Abu Ghraib were pop-
ularly interpreted—the interpretive scheme offered to the
public that helped to produce a certain understanding of the
photographs. I was saying that this interpretive framework, in
summoning responses of incredulity, then a sense of national
trauma—trauma done to the nation—foreclosed solidarity
with the victims. It revealed, if you will, the limits of our collective moral imagination. The human beings represented in
the photographs became the abstract objects of forms of torture that were considered anathema to democracy. Nude bodies piled in a pyramid; bodies compelled to simulate sexual
acts; hooded heads—who are all of these people? Can we
imagine them as workers, artists, educators, parents, children?
Can we imagine ourselves in their places? I don't think we
were encouraged to think about the images in this way. In a
sense, the public responses to the Abu Ghraib photographs
tended to recapitulate the assumptions of U.S. hegemony
that transformed the people of Iraq—and, of course, Saddam
Hussein as the quintessential inhabitant of that country—
into materializations of an ideological enemy.

I also made the point earlier that a similar dilemma can be discovered in the way historical responses to lynching—even those that vigorously opposed lynching—often tended to erase the humanity of the black victims of lynching. Thus, opponents of lynching sometimes ended up unknowingly doing the work of their adversaries.

So the dominant interpretive frame within which public conversations about torture take place in the U.S. only go so far as to reaffirm, defend, and reinforce pre-existing assumptions about the nature of American democracy—official assumptions. As a result, the very human suffering shown in the photos remains outside the discussable frame, and is thus cancelled out by going unacknowledged.

Particularly considering the extent to which American exceptionalism informs the ways in which we are urged to think about the "war on terror." This particular approach to torture affirms American exceptionalism, the superiority of U.S. democracy.

I'd like to shift gears now and begin by asking you about the usefulness of the term "Empire." Having read a lot of your work, I don't remember you using it very widely.

It is a useful term. I tend to use the term *imperialism* more than the term *empire*. As I think about the reasons I might do that, it occurs to me that I probably want to retain a very specific connection to capitalism, which is not necessary implied in the more global term empire. It is not because I don't believe it's a useful term, but rather because I want to highlight the way the current military aggression in Iraq and the Bush administration's policies of global war resonates with history, and, in particular, with the war against Vietnam. I also want to keep in mind the attendant movement of capital historically and today. The discourse on globalization sometimes conveys the impression that capital has only recently become global, and that these global migrations are a byproduct of what is called the information age. It is important to remember that capital has a long and brutal history of moving across national borders—imperialism, as Lenin and Rosa Luxemburg observed so long ago, is not a minor consort of capitalism, but rather a fundamental feature of its development. Today we refer to this era as one that is defined by the power of such international financial organizations as the IMF and the World Bank and the ability of capital not only to move across national borders, but to restructure far-flung economies, wreaking havoc on social relations everywhere. This new imperialism means that capital has entered the most intimate spaces, not only transforming people's economic activity (young girls in the Global South now produce the world's clothes and shoes)—but it has transformed their dreams of the future. This is probably why I tend to use the term imperialism.

Also, although I've been talking about the turn of the twenty-first century, it may be important to link the developments of this era with the turn of the twentieth century, the rise of monopoly capital, and U.S. imperialist adventures in Cuba, Puerto Rico, Hawaii, the Philippines. It is also important to link the role that this military aggression has played in the construction of a racial state domestically: the consolidation of Jim Crow, the industrialization of the South, the move of industrial capitalists into the Southern states in the U.S. In my own conceptual framework, I try to keep all of these historical moments in the conversation and therefore use the more processual term, imperialism.

The historian William Appleman Williams, in his very important little book, Empire as a Way of Life, *spoke of an American "imperial history, imperial psychology, and imperial ethic."*[17] *One could argue that Guantánamo and Abu Ghraib are exemplars of this imperial ethic and psychology. A psychology of utter contempt, disregard, dehumanization, and boundless hubris, on the one hand, and on the other, an ethics of impunity, asymmetry, and lawlessness. Are these not aspects of Empire as a way of life?*

Yes, absolutely. But I still insist on the acknowledgement of the fact that the putative aim of this imperial project is to guarantee the rule of democracy. And this should be perceived as a glaring contradiction: the pursuit of global dominace by military means rationalized by the defense and spread of American democracy—or should we say capitalism? I find this underlying commodification even more menacing than the hubris, which is obviously displayed by the Bush administration and which many of us accept unquestioningly. The notion of democracy has been fashioned into something like a commodity that can be exported, sold to, or imposed upon entire populations.

The imperial dimension of this project is even more obvious when one considers the extent to which rights and liberties normally associated with democracy are cavalierly subordinated to asserting superiority and control over the peoples of the entire world. Consider how elections in Iraq are staged for the consumption of those in the United States. The right to vote, of course, is represented as the quintessential moment of democracy. Therefore we were asked to momentarily suspend our memory of what paved the way for these elections—the bombing, invasion and occupation that continues to cause deaths, maiming, destruction, the dismantling of institutions, and the desecration of one of the world's oldest cultures. U.S. imperialism becomes even more menacing as it increasingly constrains our capacity to imagine what an authentic democracy might be. As the imposition of democracy is offered as primary aim of this military aggression, "democracy" loses whatever substantive meaning it might have and is confined to the formality of exercising the right to vote. This limited notion of democracy—both for the Iraq and the U.S.—forecloses notions of democracy that insist on economic, racial, gender, and sexual justice and equality.

Is it not empire also in that, like Bush the first, Bush the second has never—and could never—imagine apologizing? I mean, is not this kind of arrogance and insouciance, blatant and brutal imperial hubris?

It is. It occurs to me that there have been presidents more inclined to humility.

Like Clinton who went to Latin America to apologize for the Contras.

Or, even to take a domestic example, when Clinton apologized for the Tuskegee Experiment or tried to apologize for slavery. But it also occurs to me that the Clinton administration did much to pave the way for Bush's domestic and foreign policies. This is not to say that I would not prefer a Clinton presidency today. Of course I would, but the continuity between the policies of these two administrations cannot be ignored. And I'm not sure that it would make a major difference to have a president intent on global dominance and willing to wage war to maintain U.S. hegemony who assumed a more apologetic or humble posture in the process. Too many progressive people identified with Clinton during his tenure as president and did not recognize the need for an organized opposition. Had we responded more forcefully to the Clinton administration's attacks on Sudan and Iraq, it might have been possible to prevent the current war. And let us not forget that it was under the Clinton administration that the prison-industrial-complex began to be consolidated. It was during this period that it became increasingly difficult to distinguish between Republican and Democratic policies. Yet people who considered themselves progressive were far more willing to acknowledge Clinton as their leader. We are now in a position to draw important lessons about the failures of radical and progressive activism during that period.

I think that there is a kind of identification between the American public and the president. This is what Williams calls the imperial psychology. I mean it is just staggering that despite Bush's lying, deception, and manipulation, he manages to get reelected. When officers and presidents can trample on truth and law, as Arundhati Roy points out, we are in the midst of empire.[18] Americans reelected him. Why? Isn't this part of that imperial psychology?

A moral panic was generated by 9/11 and the subsequent specter of terrorism, which puts security at the center of all conversations, both conversations in favor of the war on Iraq and conversations in opposition to the war on Iraq. This focus on security as internal and external policing helps to manufacture the ubiquitous fear that causes people to ignore those dimensions of security that would require attention to such issues as health care, education, and housing, for example. The problem of the presidency is not primarily a question of deceit—most people, regardless of their political affiliations, and regardless of their level of education, take for granted the fact that politicians lie and deceive. That is the nature of the game and I am not sure that Bush is distinguished by his capacity to deceive. Bush was reelected precisely because of the panic generated by the September 11 attacks and because of the ease with which we were all entranced by the images and rhetoric of nationalism associated with claims of U.S. citizenship. American exceptionalism is taken for granted and there is no popular discourse that allows us to understand that the superiority of the United States is grounded in exploitation and repression.

In the aftermath of 9/11, the "nation" was offered as the primary mode of solidarity. That is to say, people were urged to seek refuge in their "Americanism," rather than to imagine themselves in solidarity with people throughout the world, including in those countries later marked as constituting an "axis of evil."

Why were we so quick to imagine the nation as the limit of human solidarity, precisely at a moment when people all over the world identified with our pain and suffering? Why was it not possible to receive that solidarity in a way that allowed us to return it and to imagine ourselves more broadly as citizens of the world? This would have allowed for the inclusion of people within the U.S. not legally defined as "citizens." The production of the nation as the primary mode of solidarity excluded those within and without who were not legally citizens. The brutal attacks on people who appeared to be Muslim or Arab announced that racism was very much alive in the U.S. and striking out at new targets. So I suppose I am more concerned about the ease with which this moral panic emerged than I am about presidential dishonesty and deception.

But more generally, as I reflect on my own political history, I can say that radical activism has always recognized that the government is not synonymous with the people. As simple as it seems, it may be especially important to emphasize this distinction today. The identification to which you referred is enabled precisely by the absence of a strong sense of community in struggle that does not have to look to the leadership of the government, especially not in times of war.

During the period before the international collapse of socialism, there existed the practice of designating those communities fighting for the rights of labor, against racism, for justice, peace and equality, as the "Other America." Today, it seems that many of us who oppose the policies and practices of the Bush administration are still, at bottom, greatly influenced by the ideology of American exceptionalism. Thus the sense of paralysis in the aftermath of September 11, and the dangerous embrace of the worst kind of nationalism. This disturbs me more than anything else, because if we are to have hope for a better future, we will have to be capable of imagining ourselves citizens of a new global order, which may well include our acceptance of leadership from people in Iraq, and from others engaged in frontline battles.

This may appear to be nostalgia for a political past that was less complicated than our present times. But actually, I am attempting to acknowledge the ways in which we sometimes tend to rely on the ideologies we think we are opposing.

One of our main challenges is to reconceptualize the notion of "security." How can we help to make the world secure from the ravages of global capitalism? This broader sense of security might involve debt relief for Africa; it would mean an end to the juggernaut of privatization that threatens the new society people in South Africa have been trying to build. It would also involve the shifting of priorities from the prison-industrial-complex to education, housing, health care. Bush was reelected—or elected, since he was appointed into his first term rather than elected—precisely because of the moral panic that diverted people's attention away from the more complicated questions about our future. Bush was elected because of the fear not only of another "terrorist" attack, but because of the fear that American global superiority may be on the wane.

I would like to ask you a question about the relationship between the production of law and the violation of law in the United States. One can't help but be disgusted by the glaring, self-serving character of some of the legal memoranda and presidential acts and rulings. Take the category "enemy combatant," and the suspension of the Geneva Conventions for people detained by the United States. The category "enemy combatant" does not exist in international law, as Barbara Olshansky of the The Center for Constitutional Rights has demonstrated.[19] Yet the term creates a legal fiction for the sake of excluding enemy soldiers and alleged terrorists from the protection of the law. These legal appeals and memoranda give the impression of legality and lawfulness. We are left with this paradox in which there is an appeal to the law in order to make exceptions to the law.

The convoluted legalistic vocabulary produced by the war on terror would make great material for comedy if it did not have such brutal consequences. These new categories have been deployed as if they have a long history in law and common usage—as if they are self-evident—and their strategic effects of circumventing the Geneva Conventions and a host of human rights instruments have once again relied on the notion that the U.S. stands above the UN, the World Court, and everything else. I wonder whether this subterfuge doesn't point to a more general problem, that of the new political discourse generated by the Bush administration. The Bush vocabulary, which pretends to express complicated ideas in the most simple and unsophisticated terms, is both seductive and frightening. It is seductive because it appears to require no effort to understand; it is dangerous because it erases everything that really matters. Just as the meaning of "enemy com-

batant" is assumed to be self-evident, so are the meanings of
the terms "freedom" and "democracy."

This leveling of political discourse to the extent that it is
not supposed to require any effort to understand—that it
appear self-evident, incontrovertible, and logical—enables
aggression and injury. This is true of the simplistic, often
crude vocabulary that Bush tends to use, it is true of his rep-
etition of the words freedom and democracy in ways that
empty them of serious content, and it is true of his representation of terrorists as "evil doers." But it is also true of such
legalistic notions as "enemy combatant" and "extraordinary
rendition."

As mentioned earlier, the term "extraordinary rendition"
describes the process of transporting prisoners to other countries for the purpose of having them interrogated. What the
term hides is the fact that the countries to which these prisoners are "rendered" are known to employ torture. As Jane
Mayer points out in her recent article in *The New Yorker*, this
is a very widespread practice.[20] This practice allows the U.S.
government to engage in torture, albeit indirectly. Again, I
would argue that the production of this kind of political discourse that obfuscates, erases, and cuts off discussion under
the guise of transparent legal jargon helps to fan moral panic
about terrorism. These terms are designed to render discourse and discussion useless. So, on the one hand, if we
analyze the Bushisms, as they have been called, they invoke
laughter and comedy, thus preventing us from taking them

seriously. On the other hand, there is the legalistic jargon that has the semblance of having been produced within established and incontrovertible frameworks of law, so they are taken too seriously. I cannot remember a time in my life when political discourse was so convoluted. We should be deeply concerned about the extent to which this tends to foreclose popular critical engagement with the policies and practices of global war.

The British Court has referred to what is going on at Guantánamo and Abu Ghraib as a "legal black hole."[21] What are the consequences of this legal black hole for human rights activists across the world?

Perhaps the lesson in all of this is that we need to find ways of contesting the absolute authority of law. We might phrase the following question: how do we use the law as a vehicle of progressive change, while simultaneously emphasizing the importance of acknowledging the limits of the law—the limits of national law as well as international law. For example, we naturally assume that justice and equality are necessarily produced through the law. But the law cannot on its own create justice and equality. Here in the U.S., thirty years after the passage of what was considered unprecedented civil rights legislation, we are still plagued with many of the same problems of inequality relating to economics, race, and gender. In many instances, they are even more entrenched in the social order. There are ways in which law can successfully be taken up strategically and thus can enable popular movements and campaigns. The focus of the civil rights movement was precisely on effecting change in the prevailing laws. But at the same time, the law produced the limits of those possible changes, as we can see in the way that affirmative action legislation has, in states like California, enabled its own demise.

The grand achievement of civil rights was to purge the law of its references to specific kinds of bodies, thus enabling racial equality before the law. But at the same time this process enabled racial inequality in the sense that the law was deprived of its capacity to acknowledge people as being racialized, as coming from racialized communities. Because the person that stands before the law is an abstract, rights-bearing subject, the law is unable to apprehend the unjust social realities in which many people live. To give a more concrete example, one that relates to the formation of the prison-industrial-complex, I would say that precisely because the law is unable to take into consideration those social conditions that render certain communities much more susceptible to imprisonment than others, the mechanism of formal due process justifies the racist and class character of prison populations. The law does not care whether this individual had access to good education or not, or whether he/she lives under impoverished conditions because companies in his/her communities have shut down and moved to a third world country, or whether previously available welfare payments have vanished. The law does not care about the conditions that lead some communities along a trajectory that makes prison inevitable. Even though each individual has the right to due process, what is called the blindness of justice enables underlying racism and class bias to resolve the question of who gets to go to prison and who does not.

While I have been referring quite specifically to the U.S. context, I would also suggest that there are ways in which human rights activists should be attentive to the questions as well. Human rights instruments can be strategic tools in the struggle for global justice. But we cannot ignore larger processes, such as the movement of global capital, which assaults entire populations. Campaigns to defend the rights of immigrants in post-colonial urban centers in Europe and the U.S. must insist on the human rights of African, Latin American, Asian, and Arab immigrants. At the same time it is important to speak out against the impact of global capitalism as a central—though not the sole—motivation causing people to move across borders. This is a major challenge for human rights activists today. And, in fact, organizations like Amnesty International that have previously focused their work at the level of individual human rights claims, have now expanded their work to defend populations and communities as well as individuals. This requires the dual strategy of taking up the law and recognizing its limitations in order to address that which the law cannot apprehend.

Earlier on you began talking about the prison-industrial-complex and the vision for an "abolition democracy"? Can you elaborate?

First, the prison-industrial-complex is a result of the *failure* to enact abolition democracy. "Abolition democracy" is a term used by DuBois in his work *Black Reconstruction,* his germinal study of the period immediately following slavery. George Lipsitz uses it today within contemporary contexts. I will try to explain briefly its applicability to three forms of abolitionism: the abolition of slavery, the abolition of the death penalty, and the abolition of the prison. DuBois argued that the abolition of slavery was accomplished only in the negative sense. In order to achieve the *comprehensive* abolition of slavery—after the institution was rendered illegal and black people were released from their chains—new institutions should have been created to incorporate black people into the social order. The idea that every former slave was supposed to receive forty acres and a mule is sometimes mocked as an unsophisticated rumor that circulated among slaves. Actually, this notion originated in a military order that conferred abandoned Confederate lands to freed black people in some parts of the South. But the continued demand for land and the animals needed to work it reflected an understanding among former slaves that slavery could not be truly abolished until people were provided with the economic means for their subsistence. They also needed access to educational institutions and needed to claim voting and other political rights, a process that had begun, but remained incomplete, during the short period of radical reconstruction that ended in 1877. DuBois thus argues that a host of democratic institutions are needed to fully achieve abolition—thus abolition democracy.

What, then, would it mean to abolish the death penalty? The problem is that most people assume that the only alternative to death is a life sentence without the possibility of parole. However, if we think about capital punishment as an inheritance of slavery, its abolition would also involve the creation of those institutions about which DuBois wrote—institutions that still remain to be built one hundred forty years after the end of slavery. If we link the abolition of capital punishment to the abolition of prisons, then we have to be willing to let go of the alternative of life without possibility of parole as the primary alternative. In thinking specifically about the abolition of prisons using the approach of abolition democracy, we would propose the creation of an array of social institutions that would begin to solve the social problems that set people on the track to prison, thereby helping to render the prison obsolete. There is a direct connection with slavery: when slavery was abolished, black people were set free, but they lacked access to the material resources that would enable them to fashion new, free lives. Prisons have thrived over the last century precisely because of the absence of those resources and the persistence of some of the deep structures of slavery. They cannot, therefore, be eliminated unless new institutions and resources are made available to those communities that provide, in large part, the human beings that make up the prison population.

If I understand your argument correctly, you are saying that the death penalty is part of the "wages of whiteness" that must be paid so as to maintain a racialized democracy, the democracy resulting from an unfulfilled abolition?

It depends on what you mean by "wages of whiteness." If we rely on Roediger's analyses, we define the "wages of whiteness" as the privileges of those who benefit from the persistence of racism. Though this may seem counterintuitive, I would argue that the death penalty is something akin to a "return of the repressed" racism of slavery, now let loose on whomever happens to be caught in its grasp, whether they're racialized as black, Latino, Native American, or white. The most compelling explanation of the endurance of capital punishment in the U.S.—the only advanced industrialized nation that executes its citizens routinely—can be discovered in its embeddedness in slavery and in the way the racism of slavery caused it to be differentially inflicted on black people. In the aftermath of slavery, the death penalty was incorporated into the legal system with its overt racism gradually concealed. In this era of "equal opportunity" it now also targets more than just the black or Latino communities. In this sense, one might argue that when white people are executed, it is more a sign of the revenge of racism, rather than the "wages of whiteness."

Let me see if I can back up and say just a few words about racism in the contemporary era, racism in the post-civil rights era, the mutations and alterations of racism, racism at a time when members of under-represented racialized groups have now been offered powerful leadership positions. How would an accessible analysis of racism address the fact that a black women, previously National Security Advisor, is now Secretary of State, and that a Latino is Attorney General? Of course this new racial integration is represented as the face of the perfect multicultural nation. This apparent dilemma can be accounted for by recognizing that racism is something that is far deeper than that which can be resolved through processes of diversification and multiculturalism. There are persisting structures of racism, economic and political structures that do not openly display their discriminatory strategies, but nonetheless serve to keep communities of color in a state of inferiority and oppression.

Therefore I think about the death penalty as incorporating the historical inheritances of racism within the framework of a legal system that has been evacuated of overt racism, while continuing to provide a haven for the inheritances of racism. This is how it can be explained that capital punishment is still very much alive in a country that presents itself as the paragon for democracy in the world. There are more than 3,500 U.S citizens currently on death row in the

United States at a time when all European countries have abolished capital punishment, when the European Union makes abolition of the death penalty a precondition for membership. Capital punishment is a receptacle for the legacies of racism, but now, under the rule of legal equality, it can apply its power to anyone, regardless of their racial background.

You mentioned Condoleezza Rice, Alberto Gonzalez, and Colin Powell as people who make it appear as if Americans live in a racial democracy. Could you elaborate on the relationship between abolition democracy and identity politics?

Of course, I am being sarcastic when I refer to the U.S. as a "racial democracy," now that we have people of color in high positions in government and the corporate world. Particular individuals are not inevitably linked to the structures of oppression implied by their racial backgrounds. Neither are they compelled to represent those who continue to bear the brunt of racism. Many years ago Dr. Martin Luther King criticized black people who climbed out of the muddy swamps on the backs of their sisters and brothers. It is inconceivable that these individuals would be where they are now, without the pressures of the movement for civil rights and racial democracy, and so it appears to be a contradiction that people of color can play major roles in sustaining contemporary racism. But, in actuality, it is more an inevitable consequence of the struggle for equality. The lesson in all this is that we need to shift our understandings of racism. In an earlier era, one of the most obvious signs of racism was the absence of people of color in governmental and economic leadership positions, which reflected more generalized forms of overt discrimination. But racism does not of necessity vanish with the appearance of individual people of color within those institutions that bear responsibility for the workings of racism. In fact, I would argue that racism is even more effective and more devastating today than it was during the era that produced the Civil Rights movement. This country's imprisoned population provides a dramatic example: among the more than two million people currently in prison, over seventy percent are people of color.

I don't know if you saw some of the confirmation hearings for Condeleeza Rice or Alberto Gonzales, but it was an incredible display of Machiavellian identity politics. In fact, you could almost talk about a Republican identity politics.

These developments indicate the limitations of the strategies of multiculturalism and diversity, which currently define official efforts to eradicate racism. Identity, by itself, has never been an adequate criterion around which communities of struggle could be organized—not even during those periods when we imagined identity as the most powerful engine of movements. Communities are always political projects, political projects that can never solely rely on identity. Even during the period when black unity was assumed to be the sine qua non of struggle, it was more a fiction than anything else. The class, gender, and sexual fissures that lurked just beneath the construction of unity eventually exposed these and other heterogeneities that made "unity" an impossible dream.

It is interesting how much more difficult it is to transform discourses than it is to build new institutions. Many decades after the fiction of black unity was exposed, the most popular assumption within black communities is that unity alone will bring progress. Even now, when we can point to the Condoleezza Rices and Clarence Thomases, people retain this dream of unity. Young people who are just beginning to develop a sense of themselves in the world assume that the only way we can make a better future for the many black people who lead economically and intellectually impoverished lives is by uniting the entire black community. I hear this repeatedly. What would be the purpose of uniting the black community? How would one possibly bring people together across all of the complicated lines of politics and class? It would be futile to try to create a single black community today. But it does make sense to think about organizing communities, not simply around their blackness, but primarily around political goals. Political struggle has never really been so much a question about how it is identified or chooses to identify, as it has been a question of how one thinks race, gender, class or sexuality affect the way human relations are constructed in the world. During Black History Month or Women's History Month, we always tend to talk about the "firsts": the first black woman astronaut, the first woman Supreme Court justice, the first black surgeon, etc. Condoleezza Rice was the first black woman to become secretary of state. As I have said many times, I would gladly give up the occasion to celebrate this as a victory in exchange for a white male secretary of state who would be capable of giving leadership to those of us who want to put an end to global war.

Can you talk about how an American democracy of false equalities and empty universals might be connected to the kind of torture, and gender diverse torturers, we witnessed at Guantánamo and Abu Ghraib?

The meaning lurking behind the model of "democracy" promulgated by the Bush administrations is the fraudulent equality of the capitalist market, the freedom it illusively offers to all. Marx exposed long ago the profound inequalities that constitute the basis of what I still like to call bourgeois democracy. But the policies and pronouncements of the Bush administration amount to a parody of even those distortions. When democracy is reduced to the simple fact of elections—never mind that they were prepared by the mass brutality and destruction inflicted on Iraq by the U.S. military—whatever we might consider to be freedom has disappeared. Those who present the gender and racial composition of the U.S. military as a dramatic example of the equality offered by democracy have clearly lost sight of whatever promise democracy might hold for the future. Gender equality in the military is represented as the equal opportunity to participate in every aspect of military life, including equal opportunity to participate in the violence previously assumed to be the purview of men. This approach to equality leaves no space to challenge the status quo. The irony that women helped inflict physical, mental, and sexual torture at Abu Ghraib is that their involvement points to the extent to which this formal, abstract democracy has been successful in the military. When equality is measured in terms of access to repressive institutions that remain unchanged or even become strengthened by the admission of those who were previously barred, it seems to me that we need to insist on different criteria for democracy: substantive as well as formal rights, the right to be free of violence, the right to employment, housing, healthcare, and quality education. In brief, socialist, rather than capitalist conceptions of democracy.

Resistance, Language, and Law

As we touched on earlier, you have been a long-time prison activist and were yourself once imprisoned. Could you tell us about your experiences in prison and how they shaped your view of the prison system itself?

My imprisonment had a major impact on the way I eventually began to think about the part played by the prison in reproducing racism and political repression. Prior to my arrest I had been active for a number of years in campaigns to free political prisoners—from Nelson Mandela and the Puerto Rican nationalist Lolita Lebron to Huey Newton and Ericka Huggins. The immediate cause of my arrest was my involvement with a case involving George Jackson and the Soledad brothers. I corresponded regularly with George Jackson during the sixteen months I spent in jail in New York and later in two different facilities in California. I would say that he, more than anyone else, urged me to think more deeply about the prison as an institution—not only about political imprisonment, but also about the relationship between the related processes of criminalization and racialization. This initiated what has turned out to be a thirty-five year engagement with the prison system. So yes, the time I spent in jail had a lasting impact on both my ideas and my activism.

We're talking about the early 1970s, with racist trials and political repression across the country, yet you were eventually acquitted in June 1972. What role do you think the activism of local and international groups played in your eventual acquittal?

Widespread national and global activism was *the* determining factor in my acquittal. There is no doubt in my mind that my acquittal was a direct consequence of organizing efforts both here and abroad. Since I have become more involved in prison issues over the last period—both as a researcher and an activist—I often imagine where I might be today in the absence of such a vast movement for my release. More than likely I would be a resident in one of California's four women's prisons in the state of California today. During recent visits to these prisons I have had bizarre flashbacks.

To give you a sense of the impact of those organizing efforts, I still have frequent encounters with people—particularly those of my generation—who speak to me as if they are meeting a long lost friend, someone they knew intimately during their youth. Sometimes this is difficult to swallow— after all they are strangers, people I am meeting for the first time. But when I tell myself that they are not really relating to me as the person I am, but rather they are encountering their own histories, it reminds me that the powerful Free

Angela Davis and All Political Prisoners campaign not only accomplished some of its immediate goals over three decades ago, but that it has also remained a signpost in the personal histories of thousands, perhaps millions of people. These people probably experience me as a pathway back to the collective political emotions of that period—and that is quite remarkable. At the time, people were touched by the campaign on college campuses, in labor unions, in churches and synagogues, as well as in social clubs and sororities.

This work also affected athletes. My brother, who was a professional football player during the 1970s, was a visible figure in the campaign—as was my entire family. His career suffered in a major way because of his leadership in the campaign. There was widespread organizing within the military. I received many letters from people stationed in Vietnam. Prisoners throughout the world wrote me to express their solidarity, even at the risk of further punishment. This movement was something so extraordinary, not only because it saved my life—and that was a major accomplishment—but also because it demonstrated that change was possible as a result of organized, mass pressure. And although I tend to resist requests by some young people who want me to tell them how they can replicate the victories of that era, I do think there are profound lessons in those historical victories. The successful coalescence of so many individuals, who came together across all kinds of differences, schisms, and borders—racial, class, political, geographical—was quite extraordinary. The creation of communities of struggle remains a major challenge today.

In addition to these schisms and borders, there was of course the daily nightmare of the Vietnam War. In what ways do you think the then-ongoing war was linked to legal and extra-legal repression of domestic political activism and liberation struggles?

Domestic political repression was linked to the war in very material ways. Consider, as an example, the 1969 attack on the Black Panther Party offices in Los Angeles, the first in a series of assaults throughout the country orchestrated by local police forces under the leadership of J. Edgar Hoover's F.B.I. Many of the police officers who conducted the L.A. attack were Vietnam veterans, including former Green Berets, who had been given special dispensation to join what was then a very new formation: S.W.A.T.—the Special Weapons and Tactical Squad. Of course, S.W.A.T. is now a household term, but the first action by a paramilitary group attached to a local police force was this attack on the Los Angeles Black Panther Party offices. At the time, we were aware that the LAPD was training Vietnam veterans in domestic counterinsurgency. As a matter of fact, those of us who witnessed the protracted assault were easily able to identify this military connection. In my autobiography, I think I described the police as "slinking along the ground" in a way that evoked soldiers in combat. Like the attack on MOVE in Philadelphia years later, the assault was initiated by an explosive charged dropped by a helicopter onto the roof of the office. I have described this incident at length because it manifested some of the more obvious ways in which military repression was domesticated and unleashed against political dissent.

Of course there was also violent repression directed against Vietnam War protestors, the most dramatic examples of which were the fatal shootings of students at Kent State by the Ohio National Guard and shortly thereafter, the police killings of students at Jackson State, a historical black college in Mississippi. Movement rhetoric was clearly influenced by our perception of the link between what we called the "war" in Vietnam and the "war" at home. This was a new take on the double "V" campaign during World War II: victory against fascism abroad and victory against racism at home. So we talked about defeating the U.S. military in Vietnam and defeating the police and other "occupying forces" at home. In black activist communities, in Latino activist communities, and especially in Asian-American activist communities, there was an overarching sense of the aggression in Vietnam as deeply connected to the rising repression against domestic struggles. However, this is not to say that the leaders of the more mainstream anti-war movement were willing to frame opposition to the war in this way. This was a thorny issue: how to participate in the anti-war movement, while opposing the strategy of treating peace as an issue unrelated to racial equality. Throughout this period, many of us fought vigorously to develop a different discourse on the war, to urge people to think seriously about the linkages between the military attacks on people in Vietnam and the economic and political repression at home against poor people and people of color.

Now we have the USA PATRIOT Act and the Department of Homeland Security as part of a rising security state. What do you think about the continuity between the forms of repression you just described during the Vietnam War and this new security state? Do you see continuity here or are we experiencing a new logic at work?

There is an historical continuity, but there are also ruptures. This continuity stretches back further than the Vietnam War era. There are definitely resonances with the anti-communism of the Cold War and there are clearly similarities with the McCarthy era. When I first learned about the USA PATRIOT Act and all of the measures used to silence people who defend the rights of immigrants who are under attack, when I learned about academics who are under fire for their resistance to the Bush administration and others who feel afraid to support them, I immediately thought about the McCarthy period. What struck me most was the extent that self-censorship not seen since the McCarthy era seemed to be occurring all over again. It seems to me that, especially now, it would be important to revisit the McCarthy era for the purpose of reflecting on the extent to which many people who considered themselves progressive and on the side of justice, were complicit in the successes of McCarthyism. Rather than openly opposing McCarthyite repression, rather than mounting a vigorous defense of those who were singled out, they were more concerned about not putting themselves in a situation where they might become targets. In this, they were further enabling the work of the House Un-American Activities Committee. By refusing to hire communists on university campuses, by expelling communists from labor unions, by actively disassociating themselves from those who were marked as the enemy, they accomplished far more than HUAC could have achieved on its own.

In the immediate aftermath of 9/11, there was a similar dynamic at work. This was especially evident during the congressional vote on the initial resolution authorizing the president to use military force in retaliation. As we all recall, Barbara Lee—who represents my district, I am proud to say—was the only person in the entire Congress courageous enough to cast a negative vote. This was a very scary moment, particularly since a number of Congresspersons—especially in the Black Caucus—indicated later that they opposed the resolution on principle, but felt obligated to vote affirmatively because they were afraid of being perceived as soft on terrorism. I am sorry to have to say this, but these are the makings of fascism.

But you are asking about continuity. I do think that there is historical continuity, but it must also be said that this is an unprecedented historical moment in so many ways. We are governed by a president who was not legitimately elected and by an administration composed of individuals who, long before September 11, 2001, had already decided that they were going to attack Iraq and to seek global dominance. Consider the Project for a New American Century. There is something qualitatively different about the extent to which those who sit in government are willing to ignore public opinion and treat mass demonstrations as insignificant. Many millions of people participated in the action that took place throughout the world on February 15, 2003. This was without precedent. Never before had so many people simultaneously gathered in so many parts of the world. But Bush acted as if only a handful of people here and there were opposed to U.S. war policies. He belittled people who tried to peacefully make their voices heard by using the analogy of "focus groups," which he would not allow to affect foreign policy.

There is something remarkably different here. I have spoken to many people who directly experienced the McCarthy era, including some who spent time in prison, and their sense is that this is a far more dangerous moment.

In this moment we have the globalization of the "war on terror" and, in turn, of U.S. detention centers and prisons that were created in attempt to be beyond the reach of U.S. and international law. What connections, if any, do you see between the globalization of these outlaw prisons and the domestic prison-industrial-complex?

The two developments are clearly related. First of all, both sets of institutions belong to the U.S. punishment system and are classified together in the Federal Bureau of Statistic's annual census. That classification includes state and federal prisons, county jails, jails in Indian country, detention centers run by the Department of Homeland Security, territorial prisons in areas the U.S. refuses to acknowledge as its colonies, and military prisons—both within the U.S. and outside of its borders. The population growth in domestic prisons, the emergence of new industries dependent on this growth, the retooling of old industries to accommodate and profit from imprisonment, the expansion of immigrant detention centers, and the use of military prisons as a major weapon in the so-called war on terror, the articulation of anti-crime rhetoric with anti-terrorism rhetoric—these are some of the new features of the prison-industrial-complex.

The prison-industrial-complex is a global phenomenon. It cannot be fully understood as an isolated development within the United States alone. What has been enabled in the U.S. and the proliferation of prison facilities and prison populations; the rapid degree to which capital has moved into the punishment industry in such a way that it is no longer a small niche, but rather a major component of the U.S. economy—all this has global implications. It recapitulates the trajectory through which military production became central to the U.S. economy. This is one of the major reasons why we choose to popularize the term *prison-industrial-complex*: it resonates in so many ways with the military industrial complex.

So the prisons, their architecture, their technologies, their regimes, the commodities their populations consume and produce, and the rhetoric that legitimates their proliferation all travel from the U.S. to the rest of the world. Why does a country like South Africa, which is in the process, we hope, of building a just society—a non-racist, non-sexist, non-homophobic society—need the repressive technologies of the supermaximum prison? Why does Turkey need U.S.-style F-type prisons? The introduction of these prisons into Turkey provoked a long hunger strike—a fast to the death—in Turkish prisons; some 100 people died as a result.

It is important to think about all of the different layers of this global process. How do we recognize that the prison in Guantánamo, for example, or the Abu Ghraib prison just outside Baghdad, reflect and extend the normalization of torture within domestic prisons? As horrendous as recent revelations about the treatment of prisoners in Guantánamo and Abu Ghraib may be, this treatment of prisoners is not qualitatively different from what happens in U.S. prisons. Take the ubiquity of sexual violence, for example—especially in women's prisons. Women prisoners in Michigan filed a major lawsuit against the state in which they argued that the government authorized prison conditions that enabled sexual harassment and assault, thus implying that the state itself was an agent of sexual violence. Human Rights Watch produced a report entitled "All Too Familiar: Sexual Abuse in U.S. State Prisons " that documents this systematic abuse. So the sexual assaults in the

Abu Graib prison confirm the deep connections between sexual violence and the gendered processes of discipline and power embedded in systems of imprisonment. These processes easily traffic between the various systems—domestic imprisonment, military imprisonment, immigrant detention. In all three sites, sexual coercion serves as a proven technique of discipline and power. The torture and sexual coercion that seems so barbaric and awful to viewers when they see it covered on *60 Minutes* is not as uncommon as it first seems, for its basis is the routine, quotidian violence that is justified as the everyday means of controlling prison populations in the United States.

Your focus on this disciplinary continuity makes me rethink the assumptions of my question, one of which concerned the importance of a legal discontinuity. The fact that these U.S.-run prisons and detention centers were beyond the reach of U.S. law, of U.S. legislators, of the U.S. media . . .

But you could say the same thing about domestic prisons.

Which then raises the question of the role of law itself. Does law really make a significant difference in this case? What about the potential for challenging these abuses? Is the existence of law in the case of the domestic prison system a potential lever, or ground, by which we can act?

While it would be a mistake to consider law as the ultimate

arbiter of social problems, it does have strategic significance in the struggle for progress and radical transformation. But law can also be one of the most difficult obstacles to change, precisely because it is assumed to be the final word. Legal challenges have indeed enabled at various moments specific reforms of the prison, but more frequently than not, these reforms have ultimately solidified the institution. Of course we must call upon law—both at the national and international level, but we should also recognize the limitations of law. The myriad legal challenges to the death penalty have not yet succeeded in abolishing it.

I would agree that we have a stake, but do we have the means of challenging the actions, if we don't have the law?

I don't know. I'm somewhat ambivalent here because I don't know whether I am willing to concede so much power to the law. In instances where there have been major victories, in the cases of U.S. prisoners, for example, those victories have been, for the most part, victories over the law—usually with the pivotal assistance of organized mass movements. Law does not operate within a vacuum. Yes, we rely on it when it can be used to accomplish what we call progressive goals, but by itself, it is powerless. It acquires its power from ideological consensus. As someone who has been involved in work against the prison system for quite a number of years, I think we need to urge individuals and organizations already committed to working against the race and class inequalities and the generalized repression produced by the domestic prison to reframe their anti-prison work in order to address and oppose the ongoing atrocities in U.S.-controlled detention centers in Afghanistan, Iraq, and Guantánamo Bay.

Bringing it back to your own acquittal, it seemed to be more a result of political organizing and the subsequent changes in the national discourse than a result of deliberations on legal grounds.

Yes, and the impact this political organizing had on the courtroom proceedings. This is the dynamic—the dialectic—I would like to emphasize.

Noam Chomsky says that the primary agent of terrorism is the state . . .

Yes, it is true. I absolutely agree with him . . .

Would you also accept that the prison-industrial-complex is one of the mechanisms by means of which the state carries out terrorism—the kind that Chomsky talks about—and that the state carries out this terrorism—prisons—under the cover of dealing with criminals?

There's truth in what you're suggesting, but it is a little more complicated, particularly given the fact that the role of prisons in U.S. society has evolved into that of a default solution to the major social problems of our times. So it *is* terror, but terror as response to an unmanageable political economy. Rather than seriously address the problems with which so many communities are afflicted—poverty, homelessness, lack of healthcare, lack of education—our system throws people who suffer from these problems into prison. It has become the institution *par excellence* in the aftermath of the disestablishment of the welfare state. So I would say state terror, yes, but it is terror for a reason. It is not gratuitous terror or terror only in response to conscious political resistance.

In your essay "Race and Criminalization" you write: "The figure of the criminal—the racialized figure of the criminal—has come to represent the most menacing enemy of 'American Society.' Virtually anything is acceptable—torture, brutality, vast expenditures of public funds—as long as it is done in the name of public safety." Do you think the "terrorist" is our new racialized criminal?

I remember that when I wrote that essay I was thinking about the "criminal" as surrogate for "communist" in the era of "law and order." I thought about this new discursive figure of the criminal, which absorbed much of the discourse of the communist enemy. In the aftermath of 9/11, the figure of the "terrorist" mobilizes collective fear in ways that recapitulate and consolidate previous ideologies of the national enemy. Yes, the terrorist is the contemporary enemy. The rhetoric, the attendant anxieties, and the diversionary strategies produced by the deployment of the figure of the terrorist are very similar to, and rely in very concrete ways on, the production of the criminal as pervasive threat.

In tracing this history from the communist to the terrorist, we also witness a change in the dynamic of race relations domestically, the relations of the African American and Muslim and Arab American communities after 9/11 in particular. What are your reflections on this change?

Before answering this question, I'd like to say very simply that racism was a significant ingredient of anti-communist campaigns. Considering the fact that Martin Luther King, Jr. was repeatedly described by his adversaries as a communist, and not because he was actually a member of the Communist Party, but because the cause of racial equality was assumed to be a communist creation. Anti-communism enabled resistance to civil rights in myriad ways and vice versa; racism enabled the spread of anti-communism. In other words, racism has played a critical role in the ideological production of the communist, the criminal, and the terrorist.

But let me try to answer your question about the impact of the emergence of this new figure of the enemy, and about the extent to which African American communities were certainly interpolated into this new racism. In the aftermath of 9/11, a new nationalist mobilization relied on the presentation of the terrorist enemy as Muslim, Arab, South Asian, Middle Eastern, etc., and for the very first time other people of color were invited into the national embrace. In a bizarre way, this was probably experienced as the reality of that multicultural nation that had been the goal of social justice struggles—Dr. King's dream, if you will—and many previously excluded communities experienced—if only momentarily—a sense of national belonging. Of course this process rested on the exclusion of the terrorist, and those bodies to whom this label was attached. We are still dealing with the consequences of that moment.

It is sometimes difficult for black people to acknowledge that it is possible for black people to be racist in some of the same ways as white people. This is a major challenge today. It is no longer possible to assume that victims of racism are not vulnerable themselves to the same ideologies that have insisted on their inferiority. There is no guaranteed passage from past radical activism to contemporary progressive positions. What is now most hopeful are the current efforts to build alliances between black and Arab American communities. At a time when black governmental leaders such as Colin Powell and Condoleezza Rice play major roles as architects of global war, these alliances will be central to the creation of networks of resistance. It is equally important to pursue alliances with other immigrant communities, especially those whose roots are in Latin America and Asia.

As with the "communist" and the "criminal," when we talk about the "terrorist," talk about their incarceration is not far behind. We've seen that Guantánamo Bay, in particular, has become a powerful symbol of incarceration. What ideological work do you think the U.S. prison at Guantánamo Bay performs?

You mean in this particular moment?

Yes.

Guantánamo has a long and ugly history. Ten years ago, the military prison in Guantánamo was employed as the world's only detention center for refugees who were HIV-positive. In 1993, Haitian prisoners conducted a hunger strike to protest their detention and vast numbers of people in the U.S. joined the fast as a gesture of solidarity. But you are referring to the outlaw military prison where initially anything was possible because the U.S. government believed that a facility that is outside the U.S. could also be outside the reach of U.S. law. Thus, the Bush administration acted as if it could act without being held accountable.

I think I'd like to use this occasion to talk briefly about the official notions of democracy that circulate today and about why activists, public intellectuals, scholars, artists, cultural producers, need to take very seriously what are very clear signs of an impending fascist policies and practices. And I use that term fascist advisedly. It is not a term that I have ever just thrown around. But how else can you describe the torture, neglect, and depravity meted out to people in Guantánamo—people who have been arrested for no other reason than that they happened to be in the wrong place at the wrong time. Children have been imprisoned for years without any contact with their families and where the highest governing officials argue that they have no right to a lawyer because they are not on the actual soil of the United States. And Guantánamo is just one U.S.-controlled hole into which people disappear. There are many.

When one takes into consideration the increasing erosions of democratic rights and liberties under the auspices of the USA PATRIOT Act, for example, it ought to be a sign that a new mass movement is needed. Fortunately, because of the British citizens who were recently released and held widely reported press conferences, we have been able to acquire a great deal more information about what goes on inside Guantánamo then we might have acquired had they not been British citizens. That the media was far more interested in citizens from the U.K. than in citizens from Afghanistan or Pakistan is extremely disturbing, since it implies that people from Afghanistan who don't carry a British passport, or Iraqi people who have been violently and sexually brutalized, are not considered worthy of media attention. I can only say that these are very frightening signposts of repressive futures that many of us are afraid to imagine. But we must confront this possibility if we feel that we have a stake in the creation of democratic futures for the Unites States and the world.

Your observation about the release of British citizens from Guantánamo seems to illustrate yet again the power of an organized public in pressuring both the U.S. and British governments, in the absence of legal mechanisms and jurisdiction, to gain their release . . .

Absolutely.

Do you think Guantánamo has displaced the supermax prison as the ultimate carceral threat in the social imagination?

Guantánamo's awful realities have material and emotional effects for all those who are unfortunate to be incarcerated there. But it is also that imaginary social environment for all those who have been labeled the enemy. Guantánamo is the technology of repression that the enemy is said to deserve. Military detention facilities such as those at Guantánamo have been enabled by the rapid development of new technologies within domestic prison sites. At the same time, new supermax facilities have been enabled by military tortures and technologies. I like to think of the two as symbiotic. The military detention center as a site of torture and repression does not, therefore, displace the domestic supermaximum security prison (which, incidentally, is being globally marketed), but rather, they both constitute extreme sites where democracy has lost its claims. In a sense, it could be argued that the threat of the supermax even surpasses that of the military detention center. I don't like to create hierarchies of repression, so I'm not even certain whether I should formulate this idea in such terms. My point is that the normalization of torture, the *every-*

dayness of torture that is characteristic of the supermax may have a longer staying power than the outlaw military prison. In the supermax, there is sensory deprivation and so little human contact that prisoners are often driven to the point where they resort to using their bodily excretions—urine and feces—as means of exercising agency and freedom. This regularization, this normalization may be even more threatening, especially since it is taken for granted and not considered worthy of media attention. Supermax practices are never represented as the aberrations Guantánamo and Abu Ghraib are supposed to be, both of which have been represented, not as normal or normalizing practices, but rather as exceptional, practices for which individuals alone are held responsible. The supermax cannot be described as an aberration. It now has the highest level of security classification within the domestic prison system. It used to be that a *minimum* implied a *medium* and a *maximum.* Now the minimum implies the supermaximum and who knows what is to come after that. But of course this is not to underestimate the horrors of outlaw military prisons.

How do you think these horrors link up with the reemergence of national discourses in the U.S. condoning torture and political assassination? From Harvard lawyer Alan Dershowitz's discussion of torture to Bush's wink and nod to Sharon and his use of assassinations, why is such talk arising now?

First of all, the Bush administration works hard to lower the level of political discourse. The gross simplification of political terms—whether through the words of President Bush or the apparently more sophisticated language used by Powell and Rice—cannot have happened unintentionally. The debasing of political discourse gives rise to extreme expressions. You're either for terrorism or against it, and if you do not approve of terrorism, then you must be against it. And if you are against terrorism, you are required to embrace all of the ideas that are put forth by the administration. This simplification of political rhetoric is, in part, responsible for the ease with which these extremist positions are expressed and adopted as normal. The challenge for us is to complicate the discourse, and to make it very clear that it is not an either/or, not a for or against situation. One can oppose the Saddam Hussein regime and at the same time be equally—or more—opposed to U.S. military aggression.

Do you think the President saying that he will get Osama bin Laden dead or alive—basically issuing a death sentence—is related to the lowering of the standards of political discourse? Do you think that this instigates the American public, and even the U.S. military, to act in more lawless and violent ways?

Absolutely. As a matter of fact, when Bush first began to talk about the "hunt" for Osama bin Laden, he announced that bin Laden was "wanted dead or alive." According to the press, individuals in some parts of the country began to shoot at his photograph for target practice and, because of the extent to which people live inside their representations, it was very easy to move from target practice to shooting down a Sikh person, who too easily became a materialization of the enemy. There were many examples of these racist misidentifications during the period immediately following 9/11.

Going back to Bush's initial "wanted dead or alive" remarks about Bin Laden after 9/11, I found it noteworthy that he avoided direct speech, invoking instead the analogy of Old West and the imagery of "Wanted Dead or Alive" posters. This calls forth resonances of the frontier, outlaw country, and the colonization of Native Americans.

What is interesting is that he may have been urging people to travel within their fantasies, because there is a disjuncture between the opposition to racism that people assume they are supposed to express—the acceptance of Native American equality, for example—and the real pleasure they experience when they watch a Western and John Wayne, or whoever it is, succeeds in killing all the bad Indians. Why are people still seduced by the fantasy represented by children's cowboy and Indian costumes? This racism is still very much a part of the collective fantasy, the collective psyche. It invites people to slip into a certain kind of regression, a kind of infantilization, so that political positions are based more on the passive entertainment people experience than on informed engagement and active involvement with issues. Lowering of the standards of political discourse encourages people to sit back and enjoy rather than sit up and think, to get up and engage. I am not suggesting that emotion must always give way to rationality, but I am saying that we need to recognize the difference. Simplistic political discourse *a la* Bush may not be so much a sign of the lack of presidential intelligence as it is a strategically important way to garner support for global war.

It lowers the gate, unleashing a flood of fantasy and fear.

What is does is disarm people. It belittles our critical capacities. It invites us to forget about criticism. I think this is one of the reasons why so many people, including progressive and radical people, in the immediate aftermath of 9/11, could not mobilize the moral resources to speak out against Bush. During the weeks following September 11, I spoke with people in New York with long histories of radicalism, and for whom I have always had a great deal of respect. I was astounded at how immobilized they felt. In many ways, people were already disarmed when Bush began to talk about "hunting down" bin Laden or that he was "wanted dead or alive."

I'd like to return to the topic of activism, if I may, and the kind of role it can play in strengthening democratic and critical practices, which might prevent this kind of politics of fantasy. What lessons might we learn from past movements of resistance and apply to contemporary struggles?

That is a very difficult question because the terrain on which organizing takes place is so different today from what it was 30 years ago. We began the interview by talking about organizing efforts around my case. There are, as I said earlier, some lessons that have contemporary resonances. Here I always add the disclaimer that this is not meant to encourage nostalgia about those good old revolutionary days—not at all. But I do think, as I've said on a number of occasions, that there is a sense today in which movements today are expected to be self-generating. There is a lack of patience. It is difficult to encourage people to think about protracted struggles, protracted movements that require very careful strategic organizing interventions that don't always depend on our capacity to mobilize demonstrations. It seems to me that mobilization has displaced organization, so that in the contemporary moment, when we think about organizing movements, we think about bringing masses of people into the streets. Of course it is important to encourage masses of people to give expression with their bodies and their voices to collective goals, whether those goals are about ending the war in Iraq or in defense of women's reproductive rights. I have always thought that demonstrations were supposed to demonstrate the potential power of movements. Ongoing movements at certain strategic moments need to mobilize and render visible everyone who is touched by the call for justice, equality, and peace. These days we tend to think of that process of rendering the movement visible as the very substance of the movement itself. If this is the case, then the millions who go home after the demonstration have concluded that they do not necessarily feel responsible to further build support for the cause. They are able to return to their private spaces and express their relationship to this movement in private, individual ways. If the demonstration is the monumental public moment and people return afterwards to lives they construe as private, then, in a sense, we have unwittingly acquiesced to the corporate drive for privatization.

Organizing is not synonymous with mobilizing. Now that many of us have access to new technologies of communication like the Internet and cell phones, we need to give serious thought about how they might best be used. The Internet is an incredible tool, but it may also encourage us to think that we can produce instantaneous movements, movements modeled after fast food delivery.

When organizing is subordinated to mobilizing, what do you do after the successful mobilization? How can we produce a sense of belonging to communities in struggle that is not evaporated by the onslaught of our everyday routines? How do we build movements capable of generating the power to compel governments and corporations to curtail their violence? Ultimately, how can we successfully resist global capitalism and its drive for dominance?

What factors do you think are mitigating community organizing today? I completely agree with the need for day-to-day orga-

nizing and community building, but not having an experiential sense of what it was like on the ground in the early 1970s, I would like to hear your reflections.

Well, you see, everything has changed, so I don't think this kind of discussion would be as helpful as one might think. Everything has changed. The funding base for movements has changed. The relationship between professionalization and social moments has changed. The mode of politicization has changed. The role of culture and the globalization of cultural production have changed. I don't know how else to talk about this other than to encourage people to experiment. That is actually the lesson I would draw from the period of the 1960s and 1970s, when I was involved in what were essentially experimental modes of conventional civil rights organizing. Nobody knew whether they would work or not. Nobody knew where we were going. I often remark that young people today have too much deference toward the older organizers, the veterans, and are much too careful in their desire to rely on role models. Everyone wants some guarantee that what they do will have palpable results. I think the best way to figure out what might work is simply to do it, regardless of the potential mistakes one might make. One must be willing to make mistakes. In fact, I think that the mistakes help to produce the new modes of organizing—the kinds that bring people together and advance the struggle for peace and social justice.

Notes

1. See Angela Y. Davis, *Angela Y. Davis. An Autobiography* (New York: Random House, 1974).

2. See Angela Y. Davis, *Lectures on Liberation* (New York: N.Y. Committee to Free Angela Davis, c. 1971 [n.d.])

3. In Joy James, ed., *The Angela Y. Davis Reader* (Malden, MA: Blackwell Publishers, Inc. 1998)

4. David Oshinsky, *"Worse than Slavery': Parchman Farm and the Ordeal of Jim Crow Justice* (New York: The Free Press, 1996)

5. W. E. B. DuBois, *Black Reconstruction* (Millwood, NY: Kraus-Thomson Organization Limited, 1976 [1935]), 506.

6. Joy James, *Angela Y. Davis Reader*, 80.

7. W. E. B. DuBois, *Black Reconstruction*, 698.

8. Here I am making reference to Jacques Derrida's notion of the democracy *avenir*. See Matthias Fritsch "Derrida's Democracy to Come" *Constellations* Vol. 9, No. 4 (December 2002).

9. Angela Y. Davis, *Are Prisons Obsolete?* (New York: Seven Stories Press, 2003), 24.

10. In Joy James, ed., *The Angela Y. Davis Reader* (Malden, MA: Blackwell Publishers, Inc. 1998)

11. Orlando Patterson, *Rituals of Blood: Consequences of Slavery in Two American Centuries* (New York: Basic Civitas, 1998).

12. Maureen Dowd, "Torture Chicks Gone Wild" *The New York Times*, Op-Ed, Sunday, January 30, 2005, 17.

13. Karen J. Greenberg and Joshua L. Dratel, eds., *The Torture Papers: The Road to Abu Ghraib* (Cambridge and New York: Cambridge University Press, 2005).

14. Sisters Inside web site is http://www.sistersinside.com.au/

15. Barbara Ehrenreich, "Feminism's Assumptions Upended" in Mark Danner, Barbara Ehrenreich, & David Levi Strauss, et. al. *Abu Ghraib: The Politics of Torture* (Berkeley: North Atlantic Books, 2004), 66-67.

16. Angela Y. Davis, *Are Prisons Obsolete?* (New York: Seven Stories Press/Open Media Series, 2003).

17. William Appleman Williams, *Empire as a way of life: An essay on the causes and character of America's Present Predicament along with a few thoughts about an alternative* (Oxford University Press, 1980), xi.

18. Arundhati Roy, *Public Power in the Age of Empire* (New York: Seven Stories Press, 2004).

19. Rachel Meeropol, ed., *America's Disappeared: Secret Imprisonment, Detainees, and the "War on Terror"* (New York: Seven Stories Press, 2004), 179-225.

20. Jane Mayer, "Outsourcing Torture," *The New Yorker*, February 14 and 21, 2005.

21. Michael Ratner and Ellen Ray, *Guantánamo: What the World Should Know* (White River Junction, Vermont: Chelsea Green Publishing, 2004), 23.

ANGELA Y. DAVIS is known internationally for her ongoing work to combat all forms of oppression in the U.S. and abroad. Over the years she has been active as a student, teacher, writer, scholar and activist/organizer. She is a living witness to the historical struggles of the contemporary era.

Davis's political activism began when she was a youngster in Birmingham, Alabama, and continued through her high school years in New York. But it was not until 1969 that she came to national attention after being removed from her teaching position in the Philosophy Department at UCLA as a result of her social activism and her membership in the Communist Party, USA. In 1970, she was placed on the FBI's Ten Most Wanted List on false charges, and was the subject of an intense police search that drove her underground and culminated in one of the most famous trials in recent U.S. history. During her sixteen-month incarceration, a massive international "Free Angela Davis" campaign was organized, leading to her acquittal in 1972.

Davis's long-standing commitment to prisoners' rights dates back to her involvement in the campaign to free the Soledad Brothers, which led to her own arrest and imprisonment. Today, she remains an advocate of prison abolition and has developed a powerful critique of racism in the criminal justice system. In 1997, Professor Davis helped found Critical Resistance, a national organization dedicated to dismantling the prison-industrial-complex, a topic that is central to her current scholarship and activism.

Former California Governor Ronald Reagan once vowed that Davis would never again teach in the University of California system. From 1994 to 1997, she held the distinguished honor of an appointment to the University of California Presidential Chair in African American and Feminist Studies. Today, she is a tenured professor in the History of Consciousness Department at the University of California, Santa Cruz.

Angela is author of many books, including: *Are Prisons Obsolete?*; *Blues Legacies and Black Feminism: Gertrude "Ma" Rainy, Bessie Smith, and Billie Holiday*; *Angela Davis: An Autobiography*; *Women, Culture & Politics*; *The Angela Y. Davis Reader; Women, Race, & Class.* Her next book, forthcoming from Random House, is *Prisons and History.*

See http://www.jcsu.edu/lyceum/angeladavis.htm.

EDUARDO MENDIETA is associate professor of philosophy at Stony Brook University. He is the executive editor of *Radical Philosophy Review*, and has interviewed, in addition to Angela Y. Davis, Cornel West, Richard Rorty, Juergen Habermas, and Noam Chomsky. He is currently at work on a book on philosophy and war.